James Wiley Magoffin

J. CISNEROS '99

James Wiley

MAGOFFIN

DON SANTIAGO — EL PASO PIONEER

W. H. TIMMONS

Professor Emeritus of History

The University of Texas at El Paso

SOUTHWESTERN STUDIES NO. 106

Art Credits:
James Wiley Magoffin by Henry Cheever Pratt, 1852.
Bachelor's Officers Quarters at Magoffinsville by Sergeant Hazerdel, 1860.
Both courtesy of the Magoffin Home.

Frontispiece:
José Cisneros's depiction of the merchant Magoffin, 1999.

First Edition
Library of Congress Catalog No 99-68186
ISBN 0-87404-282-8

∞

Texas Western Press books are printed on acid-free paper, meeting the guidelines for permanence and durability of the Committee on Production Guidelines for Book Longevity of the Council on Library Resources.

This book is dedicated to José Cisneros,
the master interpreter of four centuries of Borderlands life
and a very special friend for the past fifty years,
extending from José María Morelos to James Wiley Magoffin.

TEXAS WESTERN PRESS WISHES TO THANK
the many citizens who have made possible the publication of
James Wiley Magoffin with their financial support.
The El Paso Community Foundation also provided a generous
grant from the Texas Western Press Endowment.

CONTENTS

ACKNOWLEDGMENTS

In the preparation of this first full-length biography of James Wiley Magoffin, El Paso's best-known and most important pioneer, I am deeply indebted and extremely grateful to Jack Bristol, UTEP Professor Emeritus and Director of Texas Western Press, for his leadership, high standards, and plans for the future; to Rick Hendricks, expert on the documentary history of the Borderlands area and possessor of superb editorial skills; and to my son David, designer of the recent six-volume *New Handbook of Texas*, for the high quality that characterizes all of his work.

My thanks also go to editor Mary Anne Maier; to Claudia Rivers, Special Collections Librarian at UTEP; Lillian Martinez, head of the UTEP Library archive division; Marta Estrada, librarian of the Southwest Collection of the El Paso Public Library; Mary Kay Shannon, Assistant Park Superintendent of the Magoffin Home; the Harrodsburg Kentucky Historical Society; the Special Collections of the University of New Mexico Library; and the Texas State Library and Archives Commission.

INTRODUCTION

Fifty years ago following my appointment as assistant professor of history at Texas Western College (now the University of Texas at El Paso), I attended the first faculty meeting of the year, in Cotton Memorial Auditorium. After the introduction of new faculty members, President Wilson Elkins called on Dr. John L. Waller, chairman of the Department of History, for his committee's report on the selection of a name for the college's new auditorium.

Without hesitation Dr. Waller reported that the committee had decided the new auditorium should be named in honor of El Paso's greatest and most important pioneer, James Wiley Magoffin, Kentucky-born adventurer of sturdy and stable stock, merchant of wealth and influence, man of distinguished presence, genial host, post sutler for Fort Bliss, and dedicated servant to the Confederate cause. Dr. Waller then added that financial support for the new auditorium would be forthcoming from the Daughters of the Confederacy, and thus it came as no surprise that the motion in favor of the name Magoffin passed unanimously. It was a moment I never forgot.

In 1952 Dr. Waller published his article on Magoffin in *The Handbook of Texas*, pointing out that Magoffin became a trader in Mexico some time before 1825 and later served as United States consul in Chihuahua. He added that Magoffin made it possible for General Stephen W. Kearny in 1846 to initially occupy Santa Fe, New Mexico, without firing a shot or spilling a drop of blood. Unfortunately Magoffin's attempt to repeat this spectacular feat in Chihuahua was doomed to failure, resulting in his arrest and imprisonment as a spy for the remainder of the conflict. Receiving thirty thousand dollars from the United States government for his losses and expenditures in the war with Mexico, Magoffin built a magnificent residence at Magoffinsville, which became the center

of the social and economic life of the community. With the outbreak of the Civil War, Magoffin joined Simeon Hart and Josiah F.
Crosby in support of the Confederacy. When the Confederacy
went down to defeat, Magoffin's property was confiscated.
Although eventually granted amnesty, he died at the age of sixty-
nine before recovering his property. His son Joseph accomplished
this and carried on the Magoffin tradition of service to the El Paso
community.[1]

Dr. Rex Strickland continued Dr. Waller's work on Magoffin,
contributing new details to the story. He wrote *Six Who Came to El
Paso* (one of the six being James Wiley Magoffin), which Texas
Western Press published in its Southwestern Studies series.
Records dealing with Magoffin's early life, Strickland noted, were
scanty indeed. In 1824–25 he sailed from New Orleans, but a
tropical hurricane wrecked the ship at Matagorda Bay on the Texas
coast, casting passengers and crew ashore in the land of the
Karankawas. A schooner finally appeared that carried them to
Matamoros.[2]

Magoffin soon began to emerge as a man of substance and
position and in 1825 was named consul at Saltillo. His wife was
María Gertrudis de los Santos Valdez de Veramendi, a native of
San Antonio, whom he married in 1834. After he moved to
Chihuahua the following year, Magoffin made a trip almost every
year to the United States for goods, Strickland observed, but after
trade was prohibited in Mexico, he moved his family, consisting of
his wife, two sons, and five daughters, to Independence, Missouri,
in 1844.

Strickland thought there was no need for him to recount
Magoffin's role in Santa Fe in arranging the conquest of New
Mexico; that version of events had been told exceedingly well by a
half dozen historians, William Elsey Connelley, Bernard de Voto,
William Keleher, and Paul Horgan among them. Taken prisoner in
Chihuahua when he attempted to repeat his Santa Fe performance,
Magoffin could easily have been shot under orders from Governor
Angel Trías had he been less highly regarded.

Strickland also noted that with the thirty thousand dollars Congress appropriated for services rendered, Magoffin had returned to Independence with a view to reestablishing the Chihuahua trade, but upon arrival at El Paso he found that the customs duties the Mexican government imposed virtually destroyed any hope of profit from sales. He then settled down on the east bank of the Rio Grande, built and maintained an establishment of hacienda proportions, and served as sutler for Fort Bliss. Relying heavily on J. J. Bowden's "The Magoffin Salt War," which was published in *Password* in 1962,[3] Strickland discussed Magoffin's attempt to levy a toll upon all who took salt from property in which he had an interest. The New Mexicans' resistance to the toll was met by cannon fire from an El Paso posse, and Magoffin was indicted at Mesilla for armed conspiracy against the peace and dignity of the Territory of New Mexico.

Magoffin was a Southern sympathizer who forced the surrender of Federal properties, provided supplies for the Confederate forces of John R. Baylor and Henry Sibley, and furnished two sons to the cause. In 1865 Governor A. J. Hamilton, assuming that Magoffin's citizenship had been restored, granted him authority to reorganize the county government, but Captain David H. Brotherton, commandant at Fort Bliss, refused to allow Magoffin to act on behalf of the state of Texas. Eventually Magoffin's citizenship was restored, but he died in San Antonio on 27 September 1868 after a long illness with dropsy.

Since Strickland's *Six Who Came to El Paso*, the Magoffin years in Mexico, where he spent half of his life, have remained an untold story. In the intervening decades, however, important sources such as the Béxar Archives, the Juárez Archive, the Chihuahua archival materials, and the rich collection in the Magoffin Home became available. Now the story of Magoffin's Mexican years can finally be told. It appears in the following pages as El Paso celebrates the two-hundredth birthday of its greatest pioneer.

Chapter One

YOUNG JAMES MAGOFFIN
COMES TO TEXAS

The migration of Virginia surveyors and settlers on the Wilderness Road across the Appalachian barrier during the American Revolution marked the beginning of the westward movement in the nation's history. The first route opened across the mountains to the limitless reaches of the West, it served as the lifeline that saved the Northwest for the young republic and prepared the way for its expansion to the Mississippi River.[1]

In 1774 James Harrod led a party of Virginia surveyors and potential settlers over the Wilderness Road and founded Harrodsburg on the west bank of the Kentucky River, the first settlement in Kentucky. With the building of cabins and a fort, and the planting of the first corn crop, Harrodsburg soon became the focal point of activity for settlers coming over the Wilderness Road from Virginia. Thoroughly alarmed by this sudden invasion of British territory, Gov. Henry Hamilton, posing as the protector of Indian interests, distributed scalping knives and tomahawks with orders to wipe out the Kentucky settlements. Not until 1782 was British control broken, thus extending American rule over the trans-Appalachian region, which a treaty confirmed in 1783. By that time Kentucky's population numbered twenty-four thousand,

and in 1792 it became the fifteenth state in the American union.[2]

In the search for a market, utilization of Kentucky's central river systems was imperative. Grain and tobacco yielded large quantities of produce that had to be sold if westerners were to prosper, and the location of New Orleans at the mouth of the Mississippi River, they soon discovered, was ideal. Produce loaded on flatboats at Frankfort on the Ohio River some eighty miles northwest of Harrodsburg could be landed at New Orleans without large expenditures of money or energy. Thus, the purchase of the Louisiana Territory in 1803 opened the doors for westward expansion and the development of Kentucky into a promising commercial and industrial center in the decades to come. This naturally stimulated a healthy demand for flatboats and barges to carry goods to market, and Kentucky's farm products soon constituted two-thirds of the New Orleans trade.[3]

Carrying the produce downriver to New Orleans were young Kentuckians aboard their slow-moving broadhorns with their heavy cargoes. These young adventurers, rowdy though they were, managed to push the American frontier westward while sustaining the country's economic foundations. As Thomas Clark noted, "Kentucky boatmen may have lacked culture, but they never lacked courage. . . . they made the term 'Kentuckian' one to be physically respected."[4]

Such was the world into which James Wiley Magoffin was born in Harrodsburg, Mercer County, Kentucky, in 1799, though the exact date is still unknown. His father, Beriah, was a native of County Down, Ireland, and became a successful merchant, landowner, and bank president. James's mother, Jane McAfee, was of Scots-Irish origin, a native of Kentucky, and daughter of Samuel McAfee, a Virginia planter. James was the eldest of eight children: five sons, one of whom, Beriah Jr., became governor of the state, and three daughters. Since the family was one of substance and status, the rudiments of an education can be assumed for each child, whether at the county school, Centre College, or the family home. It was only a matter of time, however, before the young, adventurous James Magoffin left the confines of his birthplace in favor of a flatboat trip down the Kentucky, Ohio, and Mississippi Rivers to seek his fortune.[5]

In addition to the interest of the Harrodsburg Magoffins in the Mississippi River trade, two other Magoffins, possibly James's uncles, were pioneering in the frontier regions of a rapidly growing and developing nation. One was a James Magoffin, who was engaged in land surveys, sales, and development in the Mississippi and Alabama Territories in the 1815–19 period; the other was a Hugh Magoffin, who was involved in similar activities in the Arkansas Territory in 1818. Dispossessed of his land when a federal ruling returned it to the Indians, Hugh Magoffin moved south to the Louisiana Territory. By 1820 he had built a cabin and a store twenty miles west of Natchitoches and just east of the Sabine River, the boundary between the United States and Spanish Texas. Moses Austin, Texas's first colonist, was well acquainted with Hugh Magoffin's store and on his return from San Antonio de Béxar in late 1820 spent three weeks in Hugh's cabin with a severe fever. Several months later at this same cabin, Stephen F. Austin learned of his father's death soon after he had returned to Missouri. In the 1820s Magoffin's cabin and store became a major supply base and springboard for hundreds of Anglo-Americans seeking to establish colonies and build homes in Spanish and Mexican Texas. In time, reports of Hugh Magoffin's facility and the opportunities the Texas frontier offered must have reached the Kentucky region and no doubt fired James Magoffin's imagination.[6]

Sometime in the early 1820s James Magoffin and his friends, bent on adventure, took a flatboat down the Mississippi to New Orleans. With a population of forty thousand, the city was the largest and most important seaport on the Gulf of Mexico; three hundred steamboats had arrived there in 1821, along with fifteen hundred flatboats and five hundred barges. During the 1820s New Orleans became the primary outlet for the rapidly developing Texas trade.[7]

After a short stay in New Orleans, Magoffin and his friends

took an old boat out to sea but were shipwrecked at Matagorda Bay on the Texas coast. Passengers and crew were cast ashore in the land of the fierce, cannibalistic Karankawas. Some years later Magoffin recounted to his good friend, George Wythe Baylor, some interesting details regarding the unique defenses that were erected at Matagorda Bay against possible Karankawa attacks, which Baylor related in a couple of newspaper stories.[8]

> Don Santiago, as we called [Magoffin] . . . sailed from New Orleans with a miscellaneous crowd, all bent on wild adventures. Among the lot was one of Artemus Ward's profession, an exhibitor of wax works, who had Napoleon, Julius Caesar, Wellington, Nelson, and many others lifesize. . . . A hostile band of cannibal Indians held the coast country in strong force. The vessel made the bay . . . and was beached. Luckily all hands and the miscellaneous cargo of groceries, dry goods, and wax works were all landed. A fort was hastily constructed of boxes and bales, for the captain of the vessel told them that they might expect to be boiled, fried, or roasted if they fell into the hands of the cannibals. At first a strict guard was kept, and sentinels paced their weary rounds. . . . But after a while, as no Indians appeared, guard duty became exceedingly irksome, and young Magoffin on mischief bent called a convention to consider the situation, having previously arranged all the details in pure democratic style. He got up and stated the object of the meeting. That so far the burden of the campaign had fallen on the raw troops and he saw no reason why Julius Caesar, Napoleon, Washington, and the array of great military geniuses should not be made to do guard duty. The wax work owner opposed the matter and argued that his living when he reached Mexico depended on these valuable works of art, and that the exposure to the sun would ruin them. After a heated debate by young

Magoffin and a tearful rejoinder by the owner of George Washington, they compromised. It was decided that the generals and admiral were to stand guard at night, with one sentinel of the raw militia to receive their report. So Caesar and Napoleon watched the land side, and Nelson guarded an attack from the sea.

In due course of time a vessel was sighted which took them off and carried them on to Matamoros.[9]

James Magoffin had made his first trip to Matamoros in 1821, about the time that Mexico, after a long struggle, finally won its independence from Spain. This began an era of significant developments for the new nation, particularly those relating to its frontier province of Texas. In that year Stephen F. Austin, shortly after the death of his father, who had obtained the approval of local officials to settle three hundred families in Texas, formally declared his intention to continue his father's work. Although the dedicated Stephen received encouraging replies from Mexican officials in San Antonio de Béxar, those in Monterrey rejected the plan and suggested he go to Mexico City to secure the approval of Agustín de Iturbide, the liberator of Mexico. Austin then undertook the long journey to the Mexican capital and at length, in early 1823, secured the passage of a general colonization law in Iturbide's hand-picked Congress. It provided for each family interested in farming in Texas to receive one *labor* (177 acres) and for stockraisers to receive a *sitio*, or square league (4,428 acres). Naturally, most of the new colonists declared their intention to raise cattle.[10]

Opposition to Iturbide's dictatorial rule continued to grow in intensity, finally forcing his abdication. This permitted the original Congress, now restored, to suspend Iturbide's colonization law, though it allowed Austin to retain his concession as the only one granted. A short time later, the Congress passed an act on 7 May 1824 uniting the provinces of Coahuila and Texas into one state. Delegates from the entire nation met in assembly and approved a national charter known as the Constitution of 1824. It reorganized government along liberal, federalist lines, leaving the central government relatively weak, and provided the states with much greater autonomy, including the administration of public lands.[11]

James Magoffin quickly took note of Matamoros's commercial possibilities; kept watch over current political affairs; made friends with the other, more experienced merchants; and above all, gained proficiency in both the Spanish language and mercantile terminology. His activities eventually attracted the attention of a number of Kentucky and Tennessee legislators, and on learning of the availability of a consular position in Mexico, they hastened to recommend that Magoffin, in view of "his personal character, and his commercial education and pursuits," should be appointed United States consul at Acapulco, Mexico. When it was discovered that the Acapulco position had already been filled, Magoffin was appointed consul at the "port" [sic] of Saltillo on 3 March 1825.[12]

The appointment as consul was high tribute to the young man's abilities and potential, and historians have naturally assumed that Magoffin served in the position at Saltillo. Such is not the case. In 1834, having received no word from Magoffin for eight years or more, Secretary of State Louis McLane wrote him on 1 January of that year that "an examination recently made found that there is no consular bond from you as is required by Act of Congress." Then McLane wrote Magoffin again on 7 April 1834, stating that "the object of this letter is to inquire the cause of your silence and to ascertain whether the General Instructions to Consuls ever reached you."[13]

When Daniel Smith, United States consul at Matamoros, learned of the Saltillo appointment, he hastened to write the Department of State on 26 May 1834. "The emoluments of this consulate of Saltillo are deemed inconceivable as to be worthy of a person competent to discharge the consular position. This consulate should be discontinued without materially affecting the interests of our countrymen." Thus, Magoffin's abilities would have been wasted, according to Smith, if the Saltillo position had been established in the first place.[14]

In 1825 the legislature of the state of Coahuila and Texas passed a general colonization law providing for immigration agents, or empresarios, to supervise the selection of colonists, land allocation, and enforcement of the regulations. According to the law, an Anglo-American could obtain more than four thousand acres of land for approximately fifty dollars and fees, payable over a six-year period with no down payment. Since existing legislation in the United States required a cash payment of $1.25 an acre, "Texas fever" spread rapidly. Moreover, the economic depression resulting from the Panic of 1819 in the United States had plunged hundreds into debt. These people immediately viewed the Texas frontier as both an escape from creditors and an opportunity for a fresh start. A tide of immigration resulted, converting the wilderness into thriving farms, ranches, and towns. "What the discovery of gold was to California," Texas pioneer Noah Smithwick later remarked, "the Colonization Act of 1825 was to Texas."[15]

The social and economic developments resulting from the Colonization Law of 1825 convinced Magoffin in Matamoros that the commercial possibilities of the Texas trade were extremely promising. Texas products for the New Orleans market, for example, were almost without limit—principally cotton, but also wheat, corn, sugarcane, tobacco, lumber, furs, hides, beef, pork, livestock, and a variety of fruits and vegetables. There were numerous ports on the Gulf coast, such as Matagorda, Velasco, Brazoria, Anáhuac, and Galveston, that could accommodate steamboats of limited draft. Moreover, the needs of the Texas colonists were enormous— iron and steel, machinery, tools, hardware, nails, wagons and carts, furniture, ready-made clothing and shoes, and lead, powder, and ammunition. Because cash was scarce, and the counterfeiting of pesos and bills widespread, most of the trade and exchange of goods was done on a barter basis. Any merchant with a supply of Mexican silver, for example, could demand his own terms.[16]

During the late 1820s at Matamoros, the enterprising young Magoffin took note of the Texas–New Orleans commercial relationship. His keen eye quickly perceived that the older, experienced merchants employed a triangular trade arrangement involving New Orleans, a Texas port, and return to Matamoros. It began with an initial loading of silver coin at Matamoros, which was used in New Orleans to purchase machinery, hardware, and tools, all desperately needed in Texas. This merchandise was then exchanged at a Texas port for Texas cotton, which was brought back to Matamoros and sold for silver to the Mexican mill owners. Careful planning, hard work, and attention to detail, he was convinced, would almost always guarantee a tidy profit in each of the three ports. With the approach of the 1830s, the life of the Matamoros merchant seemed promising.[17]

Chapter Two

MATAMOROS AND THE TEXAS TRADE, 1825–1835

Historians of relations between Texas and Mexico in the 1830s will be forever grateful to the able and efficient United States consul at Matamoros, Daniel W. Smith, who provided most of the available information concerning the Texas trade and the vital role played by the port of Matamoros, the most important in northern Mexico. The town of Matamoros, Smith pointed out, was situated on the south side of the Rio Grande about thirty miles above its mouth. Its population exceeded ten thousand, and more Anglo-Americans resided there than in any other town. During the last six months of 1829, thirty-three vessels had entered the port, thirty-one of which were from the United States. Trade was confined almost exclusively to New Orleans, Mobile, Pensacola, and New York. Imports consisted of every kind of cotton and linen goods of British and German manufacture shipped from the United States. The article of export, he added, was silver coin from mines in the Mexican interior.[1]

With regard to the Matamoros merchants, noted El Paso writer and artist Tom Lea observed that

> Matamoros was the prettiest [of the river towns]. . . . It was also the richest, fat with trade goods, and a great

part of them contraband shipped from forwarding houses of New Orleans . . . to the mines and towns and haciendas, by busy merchants. . . .[2]

The merchants who poured the commerce at Matamoros were an assorted lot, coming in many colors, pale and deep-dyed, like goods they sold. . . .

Like the frontier that stretched out boundless about them, the merchants of Matamoros were on the make. To stay in business, they stayed sharp; if they managed to stay, they managed to get rich. The Merchants of Matamoros were the Merchants of Venice, Rio Grande style.[3]

Between the establishment, in 1825, of Stephen F. Austin's colony of three hundred settlers, and 1830, the Anglo-American population in Texas increased to more than seven thousand, twice the number of Mexicans. Lands contracted to empresarios, mostly Anglo-Americans, covered nearly all of Texas, stretching from the Sabine to the Nueces Rivers.[4] The Anglo-Americans remained apart as the Mexican and United States frontiers failed to merge. Mexican officials soon concluded that the "colonists in Texas will not be Mexican more than in name." As proof they pointed to Haden Edwards's ill-conceived revolt in Nacogdoches in December 1826 over conflicting land titles, which proclaimed the independence of Texas and the establishment of the "Fredonia Republic." Although Austin and other empresarios denounced the whole affair, Mexican officials hastened to send a high-ranking officer and administrator to study the entire Texas situation and submit recommendations for its defense and security.[5]

The appointment went to General Manuel Mier y Terán, an extremely able and perceptive soldier, scholar, and statesman, who conducted a thorough inspection of the Texas situation in 1828–29. He painted an alarming picture of the Anglo-American infiltration, pointed out with remarkable accuracy the good and bad qualities of the North American colonists, discussed local causes of discontent, and analyzed the Texans' demand for separation from Coahuila. Mexican President Vicente Guerrero's ill-advised attempt to emancipate the slaves in Texas further aggravated relations.[6]

As usual, Stephen F. Austin sought to calm the storm on 16 February 1829 by offering a practical proposal for how Texas and Mexico could work together for the benefit of both. Aware of the importance of foreign trade, Austin urged the establishment and temporary legalization of coastal trade in foreign ships. He declared that the coastal trade would forge ties of mutual interest between the colonists and Mexico and would enable Mexico to balance imports from England by exporting Texas cotton. This, however, did not come about, and the external trade was confined to the United States.[7]

Convinced that the North Americans were intent on taking all of Mexico a piece at a time, Mier y Terán in January 1830 recommended a series of strong measures for the defense of the Mexican nation. "Whatever obstacles may be encountered must be overcome," he insisted, "for these measures involve the safety of the nation and the integrity of our territory. Indeed, there is no choice of measures in this matter. Either the government occupies Texas now, or it is lost forever." His recommendations included: 1) strengthening the presidios and creating new military garrisons; 2) introducing European and Mexican colonists to counterbalance the Anglo-American influence; and 3) increasing the coastwise trade between Texas and the rest of Mexico. Austin's influence on the last point was evident in Mier y Terán's discussion of the subject.

> Coastwise trade is of the greatest importance in establishing relations with Texas, since through lack of such it is trading only with New Orleans. Cotton, one of the principal products of Texas, could be transported to Tampico or Vera Cruz in boats of Campeachy—almost the only boats engaged in the coast trade—and thence it can be carried to foreign countries. The cotton shipped out of Texas is already seeded, owing to the gins

common among the North American colonists; but
since there is no trade with the rest of our ports, it is
taken to New Orleans, where it must pay an import
duty as foreign goods. The seaports north of
Matamoros are not frequented by our coasting vessels.[8]

In addition to Mier y Terán's recommendations, which formed
the basis for the Decree of 6 April 1830, Lucas Alamán, the minister of foreign relations, inserted a momentous provision calling for
the prohibition of any further immigration from the United States.
Texas-Mexico relations fell to an all-time new low, resulting in an
avalanche of complaints and petitions for repeal of Alamán's provision. Other articles concerning the coastwise trade included in the
final version of the Decree of 6 April 1830 were: Article 1, which
stated that cotton goods excluded in the Law of 22 May 1829 could
be introduced through the ports of the Republic until 1 January
1831, and through the ports of the South Sea until 30 June 1831;
Article 2, which directed that duties received on those goods were
to be used to maintain the integrity of Mexican territory, form a
reserve fund against the event of Spanish invasion, and promote
the development of national industries in the branch of cotton
manufactures; and Article 12, which stipulated that coastwise trade
was to be free to all foreigners for four years, with the object of
turning colonial trade to the ports of Matamoros, Tampico, and
Vera Cruz.[9]

Such were the provisions concerning the coastwise trade that
Mier y Terán initiated and Alamán approved. Whether the Anglo-
American merchants of Matamoros would show any interest in
carrying Texas cotton to the Mexican ports of Matamoros,
Tampico, and Vera Cruz duty-free was, of course, highly doubtful.

In the late 1820s, about the time that Mier y Terán was com-
pleting his inspection of conditions in Texas and framing his recommendations, two Matamoros merchants, James Magoffin and
John Stryker, formed a business partnership and built a cotton gin
near the mouth of the Rio Grande. They purchased the sloop

Washington and hired a captain and seven sailors. Once equipped, Stryker and Magoffin traveled to Matamoros in early 1832 with a newly designed cotton gin and several hundred bags of upland cottonseed, distributing the seed without cost to local landowners in the Rio Grande Valley. Although the Decree of 6 April 1830 permitted foreign participation in the coastwise trade for four years, Anglo-American merchants in Matamoros shipped the cotton directly to New Orleans and paid fines on the merchandise they could sell at a huge profit in Texas. Consular documents further reveal that in the 1830–33 period Magoffin made twenty-one trips, most of them with his partner John Stryker, carrying specie, lumber, and merchandise to Mobile, Pensacola, and New York. Moreover, during those years the partnership also supplied provisions to two Mexican military units, the Presidial Company of Monclova and the Twelfth Permanent Battalion of Nacogdoches. James Magoffin had done well. In his early thirties by then, he had rapidly mastered the fine points of the Texas trade and laid the basis for the accumulation of a fortune.[10]

In late 1832 Magoffin made a trip to Chihuahua to explore the area's mining and mercantile potential, leaving his younger brother Samuel (or Manuel) in charge of operations in Matamoros. In a letter to Samuel written from Chihuahua, dated 3 December 1832, Magoffin commented on the unlimited opportunities for making money in Chihuahua, particularly if one were the owner of a ten-thousand-dollar monte, or card game, once described as a "game in which chance has more to do with the winnings and losings than in any other game."[11]

"Oh Lord," wrote Magoffin, "Chihuahua is a hell of a place as all the boys gamble like the devil. We have an English preacher here who puts his $5 or $6 down on the King for the Deuce. Oh, we have a fine lot of boys here. You Matamoros gentlemen have no idea of our commerce as it consists mostly in cards, and of all the foreigners there is not one but what goes to his death on monte every day. I believe Mr. Curcier has a notion of starting a monte. If he does I leave town."[12]

Magoffin added that he planned to visit the silver mines at Jesús María and Alamos on the way to Mazatlán to purchase goods that he estimated would bring him a profit of ten thousand to fifteen thousand dollars. Even if he did not make this amount, he said he could make it all up from "the good betting at the games. The prospects now I think are tolerably fair," he continued, "for making money if I can get hold of 10 or 15 thousand." Magoffin never forgot what he saw and learned on his trip to Chihuahua. If problems developed that adversely affected the profitable Texas trade, no doubt Chihuahua would be his next stop.[13]

Following the passage of the Decree of 6 April 1830, Anglo-Americans flooded Texas as if it had never been enacted, and by 1834 the Anglo population exceeded twenty thousand, more than double the number four years earlier. With the removal of the "paper dam," as Weber labels it, an estimated one thousand Anglo-Americans a month entered Texas, and Mexican officials began to view the tide of immigration as the first wave of a quiet United States conquest. The unassimilated newcomers continued to live apart, and many, perhaps most, viewed themselves as superior to Mexicans. The movement to separate Texas from Mexico grew, and Stephen F. Austin, who had struggled earlier to keep Texas in the Mexican union, was now giving greater support to those favoring independence. Clearly, if Mexico was still determined to hold Texas, the quickest and strongest action would be needed.[14]

In January 1834 President Valentín Gómez Farías sent Juan Nepomuceno Almonte to investigate the Texas situation and report. Educated in the United States and fluent in English, Almonte prepared a comprehensive report urging the counter colonization of Texas with Mexicans and the need for additional military support. In addition to vast amounts of information regarding the departments of Béxar, Brazoria, and Nacogdoches, Almonte offered the following suggestions with regard to commerce:

> Persons who understand such things have assured me
> that the trade now carried on between Missouri, New

Mexico, Chihuahua, and Durango, etc., amounts to
more than two million pesos. Consider, then, whether it
would not be important to open a road that offers no
great difficulties and lessens the dangers. The wild
Indians are not as numerous along this new route as
they are by way of the upper road, and the natural
topography makes travel easier, being principally across
prairies. In order to encourage sea trade between Texas
and the ports of the Gulf of Mexico, it would be, perhaps, advisable to extend the permission granted to foreigners by the law of April 6, 1830, article 12, allowing
them to carry on a coastwise trade between the colonies
in Texas and the ports of Matamoros, Tampico, and
Veracruz. Only thus will we succeed in making the
Texans build closer connections with the rest of the
republic (which up to the present they ignore) and send
their products to the interior, especially cotton, which
they now prefer sending to New Orleans, due to the
direct connections they enjoy with that port and
notwithstanding the fact that they sell it there at six or
eight per cent less than they would at Veracruz or
Matamoros.[15]

Daniel W. Smith, the consul at Matamoros, noted the deteri-
orating relations between Texans and Mexican officials and on 1
April 1834 submitted his report to the State Department with special emphasis on the coastwise trade. He began with a reminder
that the provision in the Decree of 6 April 1830 making the coastwise trade free to all foreigners for four years would come to an
end that month with little likelihood of an extension. He then
added that a rigid enforcement of required documents, such as the
guía and the *carta de seguridad*, could be expected in the immediate
future. The guía, he explained, was a mercantile passport listing
pertinent information such as the name of the merchant, number
of packages, value of the merchandise, place of destination, and the

name of the person to whom it was consigned. Failure to obtain a guía or any attempt to falsify information could result in confiscation of the merchandise, a fine, or both. The carta de seguridad, he added, was a safe-conduct pass listing the holder's physical features in great detail. It was valid for one year, cost three dollars, and could only be obtained from the authorities in Mexico City. This last requirement obviously presented considerable inconvenience, but a foreigner risked a fine or imprisonment if he failed to produce one.[16]

By 1834 Magoffin, then thirty-five, was an experienced Matamoros entrepreneur whose knowledge of the mercantile trade, proficiency in Spanish, and accumulation of wealth had gained the respect of Mexican officials who addressed him as Don Santiago. Others who had learned of his consular appointment referred to him as Consul Magoffin. Moreover, his marriage in 1834 to María Gertrudis de los Santos Valdez de Veramendi, daughter of the prominent and influential family of San Antonio de Béxar, gave him additional status. Her brother, Gabriel Valdez, was a trader on the Santa Fe Trail, and her cousin, Manuel Armijo, was a rich, self-made merchant from Albuquerque who became governor of New Mexico.[17]

In mid-1834 General Antonio López de Santa Anna overthrew the liberal government of Valentín Gómez Farías. He immediately announced his determination to increase the size and strength of military forces in Texas, reorganize the customhouses, and demand the strict enforcement of all Mexican laws and regulations. He appointed his brother-in-law, Martín Perfecto de Cos, as commandant general of the Eastern Interior Provinces headquartered in Matamoros, and Colonel Domingo de Ugartechea as commandant of Texas, with headquarters in San Antonio de Béxar. In January 1835 Don José González arrived in Anáhuac to reopen the customhouses, closely followed by a detachment of soldiers under Captain Antonio Tenorio, who had come to enforce collection of all customs duties. To Don Santiago Magoffin, merchant of Matamoros, it was clear that the period of prosperity he had enjoyed in Texas was rapidly coming to a close. By March 1835 he had made his decision to leave Matamoros and return to Chihuahua.[18]

In compliance with Mexican regulations, Magoffin prepared his merchandise for shipment to Chihuahua in four separate guías. Most of it consisted of cotton goods and fabrics packaged in 189 parcels and valued at more than forty-eight thousand pesos. The merchandise was to be shipped by mule train escorted by a *caballada*, or horse herd, across the forbidding Bolsón de Mapimí for delivery within sixty days to Don José Cordero of Chihuahua. The *derecho de consumo*, or 5 percent excise tax, amounted to 2,441 pesos. Details regarding the merchandise shipped are given in the following table.[19]

MERCHANDISE	PURCHASE PRICE (pesos)	CURRENT VALUE (pesos)	TAX (pesos)	No. OF PARCELS
Guía 1, Cotton Goods	5,916	14,937	747	54
Guía 2, " "	711	17,956	897	74
Guía 3, " "	3,917	9,892	494	38
Guía 4, " "	2,403	6,069	303	23
Totals	12,947	48,854	2,441	189

During the month of May 1835, Mexican officials in Matamoros, Béxar, and Anáhuac, unaware of Magoffin's departure, conducted a voluminous correspondence concerning his shipment of goods from New Orleans to Texas without the required payment of duties and in violation of the regulations. All this became academic, however, with the receipt of information that Magoffin's merchandise with the four guías had arrived on 17 May 1835 at the town of Guerrero, just west of Chihuahua, where James Magoffin and his family had their home and headquarters for the next eight years. Brother Samuel remained in Matamoros until 1839.[20]

Chapter Three

THE CHIHUAHUA TRAIL, 1835–1846

A major development on the New Mexican frontier in 1821 was the opening of the Santa Fe trade by William Becknell, who brought back his mules, loaded with rawhide bags of silver, to Franklin, Missouri, in 1822. Later that year, according to Josiah Gregg, seventy men supplied with pack animals and three wagons carried goods valued at fifteen thousand dollars to Santa Fe, of which a portion worth nine thousand dollars went on to Chihuahua. In view of Chihuahua's population, which was twice that of Santa Fe; its extensive mining operations; and a mint that annually issued more than five hundred thousand dollars in coin, the city held promise of eventually replacing Santa Fe as "the principal emporium of the overland trade." By 1846 the volume of trade involved 750 men and 363 wagons carrying goods worth a million dollars to Santa Fe, most of it sold in Chihuahua and other interior towns. Profits were generally about 50 percent, and sometimes as much as 100 percent, but the risks were always great.[1]

Edward J. Glasgow, a veteran of the Chihuahua trade in the 1840s, described it in detail.

> The goods dealt in were largely of brown and bleached cotton manufactures and printed cottons or calico—

some few silk goods and woolen cloth and cassimires
were included and the usual assortment of articles sold
in dry goods stores, but the great bulk of the trade was
in cotton goods. Up to the time of our war with Mexico
those goods were sent in steamboats to Independence,
Missouri, and there loaded in wagons of large size and
generally drawn by eight or ten mules. . . . No white
people lived on the road. . . . The plains were occupied
by many tribes of Indians. . . . In New Mexico and
Chihuahua the Apaches roamed and constant vigilance
was necessary to protect the traders mules, there and on
the plains from the Indians thieving.[2]

The silver bars brought back from Mexico weighed between
fifty and eighty pounds each and were valued at a thousand to two
thousand dollars. As a result, noted Max L. Moorhead, the overland trade generated a stabilizing effect on the monetary system of
Missouri. "We brought back silver," Glasgow added, "in $5000
packages we made by skinning an ox and sewing the silver up in the
green hide. Then we left it in the sun to dry. When the sun had
shrunk it down on the metal, the only way to get at the money was
with an ax. . . . With a team of ten mules to the wagon, it generally took about three months and a half to make the trip between
Independence and Chihuahua."[3]

Documents in state and local archives in Chihuahua reveal
that during the 1840s some fifty Anglo-Americans were engaged in
mining, merchandising, or some combination of the two, largely
concentrated in Chihuahua, Corralitos, and El Paso del Norte.
Many played significant roles in Chihuahua affairs; one was James
Magoffin, the merchant of Matamoros, who became one of the
great names on the Chihuahua Trail.[4]

In 1835 the Santa Anna government established a custom-
house in El Paso del Norte for the inspection of cargoes, seizure of
contraband goods, enforcement of prescribed procedures and
regulations, and collection of custom duties on all merchandise

coming from Santa Fe. Although it appears that the El Paso customhouse was managed more efficiently than the one in Santa Fe, Magoffin on one occasion claimed that the Mexican officials there had cheated his brother Samuel by adding ciphers to the value of some imported merchandise, thus increasing the amount of the duty by $355. When Magoffin filed a complaint with the United States consul in Mexico City, the only result was a request for further documentation, which Magoffin said would cause him considerable personal inconvenience and expense. He added that there was no way anyone could check the merchandise delivered to Jesús María because Apaches held the town.[5]

The presence of Magoffin and the other Anglo-Americans involved in the Santa Fe–Chihuahua trade concerned Mexican officials greatly, particularly because they suspected them of violating a Chihuahua law prohibiting "the sale of arms, ammunition, and alcohol" to Apaches. The *jefe político* of El Paso del Norte reported to his superior in Chihuahua that Anglo-Americans in great numbers had entered the territory of New Mexico with mule trains, caused at least one stampede near Fray Cristóbal, violated and ridiculed Mexican laws and regulations, and stolen livestock and manipulated the brands. One of these Anglo-Americans, the jefe político said, was named Don Santiago. He had an extensive copper trade in Chihuahua, the official continued, and encouraged his Anglo-American friends to provide arms and munitions to Apaches and Comanches to pacify them so they would not interfere with the trade between Santa Fe and Chihuahua.[6]

Stephen Courcier (or Esteban Curcier, as he signed), of French descent and a native of Philadelphia, was Magoffin's principal associate in Chihuahua. He had leased the richest mine in Chihuahua, Santa Rita del Cobre, on the Gila River, from a representative of its owner, the Elguea family of Chihuahua. Between 1828 and 1835, Curcier leased the mine; secured the permission of the aged chief, Juan José Compá; gained control of the Chihuahua mint; flooded the country with copper pesos; fixed prices; and made a profit of half a million dollars. Shortly after Magoffin arrived in Chihuahua in 1835, he joined Curcier as a partner and supplied both the Santa Rita and Corralitos mines and the presidio of Janos with fabrics, clothing, dry goods, and hardware. Under the new leadership of Mangas Coloradas, an Apache, however, Indian hostilities resumed with a vengeance, and Curcier and Magoffin were forced to abandon their operation at Santa Rita and shift their activities to the Barranco Colorado and Veta Grande mines near Corralitos.[7]

In the 1840s the government of Chihuahua named John Potts, an Englishman, chief proprietor of the Chihuahua mint. At his direction, the 1830s' policy of accepting only copper was discarded, and the mint began again receiving silver and gold, as well as copper, for coinage purposes. "There is a well-managed mint (casa de moneda) in Chihuahua," wrote the German physician Dr. A. Wislizenus,

> coining gold, silver, and copper. Mr. J. Potts and
> brother are the present proprietors, in consequence
> of a contract made with the government of Chihuahua.
> As all the silver ore in the State contains more or less
> gold, they separate it before coining, in large platina
> vessels, with sulphuric acid. For coining a marc of silver
> without separating the gold, they receive two reals (25
> cents); for coining and separating the gold, five reals;
> but the marc of silver from which the gold is to be sepa-
> rated must contain at least 16 grains of gold.[8]

In an effort to solve its Indian problem, the state of Chihuahua enacted a barbarous law in 1837, the Proyecto de Guerra, that offered a bounty on Indian scalps. James Johnson led a party of scalp hunters intent on exterminating the entire tribe of Mimbreño Apaches living near the Santa Rita mine. They invited the Apaches to a fiesta, and after the Indians had eaten and drunk their fill, four hundred of them, men, women, and children, were massacred. The Apaches retaliated. They starved the miners by severing all lines of communication, set fire to the supply wagons, flooded the mine shafts, and ambushed survivors who were attempting to escape to Janos Presidio. All efforts to recapture the mine failed, and it remained closed during the 1840s. It was clear that unless the Apache problem could be brought under control, Magoffin was left with an uncertain future.[9]

Magoffin's correspondence of 1838–39 to the United States consul in Mexico City indicates that he had experienced "many ups and downs" and that an entire year spent on the Pacific coast had brought him only "a total disarrangement of his affairs." He added that he had faced "many difficulties of a pressing nature," but had somehow managed to keep his "head above water." Finally, he asked the consul to remit to the Mexican government an enclosed list of cartas de seguridad, inasmuch as most of his countrymen had been fined twenty dollars each for failing to produce their cartas for 1838.[10]

In an effort to shorten their trade route, in 1839 James Magoffin and his friend and fellow merchant, Henry Connelly, loaded seven hundred mules in Chihuahua and drove them across Texas to St. Louis. They then loaded eighty wagons of goods for the return trip the following spring. After spending five months trying to cross the rain-swollen Red River, they finally reached the open prairies, but it was another three before they completed the round trip to Chihuahua. From that time on, the Chihuahua traders used the traditional route by way of El Paso del Norte and Santa Fe.[11]

In the meantime, Apaches had greatly intensified their raids on Chihuahua, and to make matters worse, Comanches were increasing their offensive operations. With Chihuahua's defenses in ruins and its economy a shambles, it was only a matter of time, officials concluded, before Apaches would be camping outside the capital, leaving merchant activities completely paralyzed. A helpless and desperate Chihuahua government again recruited foreign mercenaries to solve its problems.[12]

Chihuahua officials enlisted the services of Santiago (James) Kirker, an Irishman turned Mexican, offering him one hundred thousand pesos to bring the Indian problem under control. Known as "the king of New Mexico," Kirker, a trapper, hunter, and explorer, was the equal of the Apaches in marksmanship, horsemanship, treachery, and torture. The party of scalp hunters he led over the next two years collected a large bounty in Chihuahua. In support of Kirker's offensive against Apaches, the Chihuahua government established La Sociedad de Guerra contra los Bárbaros (The Society for War against the Barbarians) and named Curcier as president.[13]

The Apache problem forced Magoffin to suspend his mercantile operations for eighteen months during 1841 and 1842, a period he spent as a member of the Ayuntamiento de Chihuahua. Since he held the office of president of that body on several occasions, some Mexican officials assumed he was a naturalized Mexican citizen, although to date no official records have been found to support this. Moreover, some Mexicans noted that the Magoffin family did not hesitate to provide assistance for the survivors of the Texan–Santa Fe Expedition of 1841, which Mexican officials considered a flagrant Texan invasion of Mexican territory.[14]

By late 1841 the Mexican government had concluded that Kirker's exploits were counterproductive since both Apache and Comanche raids were on the increase. Kirker was retired, but he soon joined his former adversaries as the "Chief of the Apache Nation." As a last resort, Commandant General Francisco García Conde of Chihuahua called for an Apache policy of all-out peace. This led to the signing of a number of peace treaties with Apache groups in 1842, with the Mexican government providing a rations program as it had in the 1820s.[15]

Tensions between Anglo-American merchants and Mexican officials mounted in the 1840s, resulting in a decree in 1843 that closed the frontier customhouses and ordered a halt to the overland trade with the United States. So great was the opposition of Anglo-American merchants that many feared a serious outbreak of violence. As it turned out, the decree was repealed the following year, but another law was passed in 1844 prohibiting foreigners from engaging in retail trade unless they were naturalized citizens, married to Mexicans, or resident in Mexico with their families. The Anglo-American merchants who had arrived only a short time before were most affected. They argued that they were being forced to accept Mexican citizenship involuntarily and were being preyed upon by capricious and tyrannical Mexican officials interested only in obtaining bribes. Although the law was repealed, the merchants continued to feel frustrated in the absence of a United States consul to articulate their grievances. In view of the increasingly strained relations between the United States and Mexico, what they feared most was a war between the two countries. Given the extensive American economic involvement in Chihuahua, it was more than likely that in the event of war Chihuahua would be a major area of conflict. Losses in the millions of dollars could be the result.[16]

Although Magoffin must have had serious misgivings about the conditions in Chihuahua regarding Anglo-American merchants, his decision to return to Missouri in 1844 was based on his desire for his seven children to receive their education in the United States. By this time Samuel was nine, Joseph was seven, and two of his five daughters, Josephine and Ursula, were approaching school age. After the death of his wife at Independence in January 1845, sons Samuel and Joseph were sent to school at Lexington, Kentucky, and Josephine and Ursula entered the Convent of the Visitation in St. Louis. The three younger girls, Annetta, Angela, and Gertrudis, were placed in the care of their maternal aunts.[17]

By the 1840s the principal center for the organization of merchant trains for the Santa Fe and Oregon Trails was Independence, seat of Jackson County, Missouri, located five miles east of Kansas City. A town of seven hundred residents in the 1840s, Independence boasted several general stores, blacksmiths, wagonmakers, saddle and harness shops, druggists, jewelers, hatters, gunsmiths, and tinners. With the growth of Westport and Kansas City during this period, however, Independence declined as an outfitting center, largely because it was not on the Missouri River.[18]

Magoffin's first act after his return to Missouri was to establish a farm for breeding mules to be used in the trade between Independence and Santa Fe. He acquired the 258-acre estate, situated astride the road that led from Blue Mills Landing on the Missouri River to Independence, in 1843. Four years later, after a total outlay of five thousand dollars, he became the sole owner. The next year he sold the farm to his younger brother Samuel and his new bride, Susan Shelby, for six thousand dollars.[19]

The annexation of Texas in 1845 led to the breaking of diplomatic relations between the United States and Mexico. In August, as war became imminent and the likelihood of a United States invasion of the Mexican frontier grew to be a real possibility, Angel Trías, whose anti-American sentiments were well known, became governor of Chihuahua. Trías, a well-educated, wealthy *hacendado*, enjoyed great popularity because of his dedication to the interests of the state. Learning of the United States's annexation of Texas, Trías called for registration of all males eighteen years and older and the organization of military battalions. He also urged towns to take all possible steps to defend the nation. With the United States's declaration of war against Mexico on 13 May 1846, a Mexican official wrote:

> [Governor Trías] has displayed the energy and activity which might be expected from his genius and patriotism. He takes not a moment's repose. He has reanimated public spirit. All is action and movement among the citizens, who hurry to enrol themselves on the registers. But we want everything, everything. There is no powder—there are not arms enough, and the few that we have are much out of order; there is no lead; there is no copper, nor pieces of artillery; there is no money, and, finally, no time to create resources, and prepare for a regular resistance, for men cannot perform miracles.

Notwithstanding this, I do not believe that the same thing will happen here, which has happened in New Mexico.[20]

Following the declaration of war, more than three hundred Anglo-American wagons, worth at least a million dollars, were heading westward along the Santa Fe Trail. One caravan belonged to Samuel Magoffin and his new bride, Susan; James Magoffin owned a second, which his brother-in-law, Gabriel Valdez, and a younger Magoffin named William supervised. Other prominent merchants involved were Dr. Henry Connelly; Edward J. Glasgow; Francis McManus; several Mexicans; and the Manuel X. Harmony, Nephews and Company, which was transporting more than thirty-eight thousand dollars in goods in twelve wagons.[21]

The caravan belonging to Samuel and Susan Magoffin consisted of fourteen large, ox-drawn wagons filled with trade goods; a baggage wagon; a dearborn and a carriage carrying Samuel Magoffin and Mr. Hall, the wagonmaster, as well as Susan and her maid; two hundred oxen; nine mules; two riding horses; and the Magoffins' greyhound, named Ring. In all there were forty-five wagons.[22]

The *Missouri Republican* of St. Louis reported from Independence on 16 May that the scene in town had recently changed in notable ways:

> Instead of a great bustle of emigrants for Oregon
> and California, with their wagons crowding our streets,
> laying in their outfits for their journey across the plains,
> we have a great crowd of Mexicans and traders going to
> Santa Fe and Chihuahua. It is supposed that we have
> two hundred Mexicans in the town and vicinity, at this
> time. [One group] arrived here a few days in advance
> of the main company, making the trip from Chihuahua
> in forty-six days. The present week several companies
> have arrived. . . . [they] are on their way to the east to

purchase goods. They came in the early part of the week; also, James Magoffin, with others from Chihuahua, have reached here. These various companies have brought in an immense quantity of specie, amounting to about $350,000. . . .

About forty wagons have left for Santa Fe and Chihuahua this week, and others are preparing to leave shortly. The late war news from Mexico does not seem to intimidate the traders.[23]

Magoffin had returned from Chihuahua to Independence, Missouri, on 21 May with forty thousand dollars and there found Senator Thomas Hart Benton's note urging him to come to Washington at once. Three weeks later Magoffin arrived in the nation's capital. Senator Benton was taken with him, writing that Magoffin was "a man of mind, of will, of generous temper, patriotic, and rich. He knew every man in New Mexico and his character, and all the localities, and could be of infinite service to the invading force." Benton introduced Magoffin to President James K. Polk as a man of considerable expertise on northern Mexico, at ease in Spanish and with many friends in Chihuahua and New Mexico. President Polk, extremely impressed with Magoffin, wrote letters in his behalf and ordered him to join Colonel Stephen W. Kearny's army on its way to New Mexico, where the colonel hoped to persuade Governor Manuel Armijo to surrender without a fight.[24]

On 18 June 1846 the secretary of war, William L. Marcy, wrote Colonel Kearny the following letter concerning Magoffin.

At the request of the President I commend to your favorable consideration the bearer hereof, Colonel James W. Magoffin. Mr. M. is now and has been for some years a resident of Chihuahua and extensively engaged in trade in that and other settlements of Mexico. He is well acquainted with the people of

Chihuahua, Santa Fe and immediate country. He was introduced to the President by Col. Benton as a gentleman of intelligence and a most respectable character. The President has had several interviews with him and is favorably impressed with his character, intelligence and disposition to the cause of the United States. His knowledge of the country and the people is such as induces the President to believe he may render important services to you in regard to your military movements in New Mexico. He will leave here for Santa Fe immediately and will probably overtake you before you arrive at that place. Considering his intelligence, his credit with the people and his business capacity, it is believed he will give important information and make arrangements to furnish your troops with abundant supplies in New Mexico. Should you apprehend difficulties of this nature it is recommended to you to avail yourself in this respect and others of his services for which he will as a matter of course be entitled to a fair consideration.[25]

Chapter Four

MAGOFFIN'S NEGOTIATIONS ON THE CHIHUAHUA TRAIL, 1846–1848

I mmediately following Magoffin's interview with President Polk, he was commissioned as a colonel of cavalry, provided with letters of recommendation, and sent to Bent's Fort for future assignment. The letters, one to Colonel Kearny and another to General John Wool (who had been assigned to march on Chihuahua), indicated that the president thought Magoffin could render "important services" to the military operations, given his intelligence, patriotism, and knowledge of northern Mexico. At Bent's Fort on 31 July, Kearny declared that his army had come in peace for the sole purpose of occupying the territory. Then, on 2 August, Kearny ordered Magoffin and Captain Philip St. George Cooke, with an escort of twelve dragoons under a flag of truce, to confer with Governor Manuel Armijo in Santa Fe. José González, one of Magoffin's business associates, accompanied the group as interpreter. Cooke was given a letter from Kearny stating that the objective of the United States was to take possession of that part of New Mexico lying east of the Rio Grande, which it claimed as a part of Texas. He and his army were coming in peace, the letter stated, and any bloodshed would be Armijo's responsibility.[1]

The Cooke expedition, known as the Army of the West, consisted of a regiment of cavalry, two batteries of horse artillery, and a battalion of infantry, a total of seventeen hundred personnel. It took the short, steep mountain route to Raton, New Mexico. Cooke, who kept careful notes, reported at the end of the second day that Magoffin was in a better mood than on the first. "Reclining on the grass, after lunch," he wrote:

[Magoffin] made a long speech to Gonzales, in the most sonorous Spanish, about liberty and equality, and the thousand advantages of being conquered by our arms. Then, chuckling, he swore the old rascal would get himself in the calaboose as soon as he got to Chihuahua. He then held up, and addressed a pocket cork-screw, which, he said he had carried for eight years. "You have cost me a thousand—five thousand dollars; but what do I care except for a bottle of wine every day; I work this way on purpose to keep you; what is money good for? I would not say to a bottle of champagne, 'I won't, I cannot use you,' for a million of dollars. I travel this way every year over deserts just to be able to have my wine and educate my children. I will educate them as long as they can stand it; give them all sorts of teachers, to teach them all they can pound into them, and when they say 'we have beaten into their heads all that we *possibly* can,' then I will be satisfied; that is all I want to do for them."[2]

Captain Cooke wrote that "the view from the top of the mountain is very extensive—very fine; it embraces not only the Spanish peaks, but Pike's Peak," more than one hundred miles to the north. "The descent was long and rough," Cooke continued, "but Don Santiago's claret was very welcome again." On 8 August Cooke and Magoffin rode to the home of the alcalde of Las Vegas, an old acquaintance of Magoffin. The neighbors dropped in, and there were drinks and festivities. Cooke later learned that the alcalde sent details about the occasion to the governor at Santa Fe. On 11 August the expedition arrived at a walled town called Pecos situated on a hill between two branches of the Pecos River. "Here we see partially ruined temples of two religions which met in rivalry," noted Cooke, "the Aztec with unceasing altar fire, and that of Rome with its graven images." As they approached Santa Fe, Cooke wrote that his stomach was refusing everything, but added, "Don Santiago gave me a little claret wine which he had kindly insisted on putting within my reach."[3]

Negotiations between Kearny and Governor Armijo began on 12 August. According to Cooke, Armijo seemed to be in "painful doubt and irresolution, halting between loyalty to his army commission and his desire to escape the dangers of war upon terms of personal advantage." Kearny then instructed Magoffin to meet Armijo that night, and in an all-night session Magoffin worked to convince the governor of Kearny's peaceful intentions and the folly of resistance. Magoffin could see, however, that Armijo had not been entirely won over, for Colonel Diego Archuleta, the governor's second-in-command, had a thousand troops ready and was determined to resist. This led to a private meeting between Magoffin and Archuleta and a promise to Archuleta that if he would lay down his arms, he might well seize the territory west of the Rio Grande for himself.[4]

Just when it appeared that Kearny's forces were in a position to take New Mexico without resistance and bloodshed, Armijo, on 14 August, denied the legality of the U.S. claim to New Mexico. He asserted that he had more than enough forces for a successful resistance and stated that the people had rallied in support of his leadership. He quickly mobilized three or four thousand men at Apache Canyon, about fifteen miles from Santa Fe, and by 16 August they were at full strength. Kearny, who could not assume that Armijo was bluffing, dispatched his own force of sixteen hundred men and sixteen pieces of artillery in the direction of the canyon. Then, just as suddenly, Armijo told the militia at Apache

Canyon that he could not risk a battle using people lacking military training, and his army quickly began to melt away. But a fee of from twenty to a hundred dollars was charged each man who decided to return home! Armijo then declared that his militia had deserted him. With the way to Santa Fe clear, on 18 August Kearny's Army of the West entered Santa Fe unopposed.[5]

In Magoffin's report to Secretary of War Marcy on 26 August 1846, he made no claim that he alone was responsible for the peaceful occupation of Santa Fe. He pointed out that Kearny's proclamation of 31 July had greatly influenced the decision of Armijo's officers not to fight. Magoffin wrote:

> Armijo left this place [Santa Fe] early on the 16th with 150 Dragoons and joined his army called his officers together and sought to ascertain if they were prepared to defend the territory. They answered that they were not, that they were convinced by the proclamation they had from Genl. K[earny] that the U.S. had no intention to wage war with New Mexico, on the contrary, [he] promised them all protection in their property, person and religion. Armijo . . . gave orders for the troops to be dispersed.[6]

For many years writers have assumed that Magoffin played the key role in Kearny's conquest of New Mexico, mainly because of an all-night champagne session he hosted for Governor Armijo, who succumbed to his "inducements." This assessment is based principally on Magoffin's letter of 4 April 1849, written in support of the largest possible payment of U.S. government funds for the services he had rendered in the war with Mexico. In the letter he stated that he had gone to Santa Fe ahead of Kearny to prepare the way for the surrender of New Mexico's capital without a fight.[7]

It should be noted, however, that even if Magoffin was not the most significant actor, his contribution was still important. Writing on 14 January 1849, Henry Smith Turner commented to Magoffin that

> Having been Chief of Gen. Kearny's Staff when he entered New Mexico in 1846 at the head of the Army of the West, I distinctly remember the services rendered by you to the Government, and to the General, in enabling the latter to accomplish successfully the object of that expedition: viz. the conquest of New Mexico *without bloodshed, or resistance on the part of the inhabitants.* This was much desired by our Government at the time; and I have no hesitation in saying, that the General was greatly aided in bringing it about, by your acquaintance with, and the influence you exercised over, the leading men of the Country.[8]

With regard to Kearny's conquest, Howard Lamar espoused the view that became traditional, that General Kearny had accomplished what Polk, Benton, and all Missourians wanted by conquering New Mexico without firing a shot, but he also noted that the real conquest had taken thirty years and had been the work of traders and merchants such as James Magoffin, Manuel Alvarez, Henry Connelly, Ceran St. Vrain, and Charles and William Bent. For Lamar, conquering New Mexico "meant regularizing and securing rich trade and safe transportation routes for a previously erratic, uncertain enterprise. It was, in short, a conquest of merchants who worried little about extending the glories of free government to their captive customers."[9]

In the wake of his experience in New Mexico, Magoffin could logically assume that he could win Chihuahua in the same manner, through negotiation and persuasion rather than by force of arms. If satisfactory arrangements could be made with the Chihuahua officials, business would return to normal, again bringing profits for both Anglo-American and Mexican merchants. Magoffin thus hoped to convince his many influential friends in Chihuahua that they had as much to gain by negotiating a settlement as the Americans did. At her home in Santa Fe on 31 August, Susan Magoffin wrote that "brother James is to start for Chihuahua tomorrow."[10]

James Magoffin and party began their march down the Rio Grande in early September 1846, confident that an arrangement could be made with Mexican officials and peace restored for the benefit of all. Yet on 27 September Sebastián Bermúdez, the prefect of El Paso del Norte, reported that the *juez de paz* of Doña Ana had detained Don Santiago Magoffin, a naturalized Mexican citizen, and four others, ordering them taken to El Paso del Norte under escort. They were placed under arrest there while the juez of El Paso del Norte decided their final disposition. The Apaches at Brazito had carried off all Magoffin's wagons, equipment, and papers, said Bermúdez, but they were recovered and inventoried in El Paso del Norte. Henry Connelly and Francis McManus were captured with Magoffin, and since Mexican officials were highly suspicious of them, they were all sent under heavy guard to be imprisoned at Carrizal Presidio.[11]

On 1 December Susan Magoffin wrote:

> News comes in very ugly today. An Englishman from
> Chihuahua, direct, says that the three traders, Dr.
> Conley, Mr. McMannus and brother James . . . have been
> taken prisoners, the two former lodged in the calaboza
> while Brother James is on a *trial for his life*, on account of
> his interview with Armijo at Santa Fé, which they say was
> one cause of the latter's having acted as he did in regard
> to the American Army—and also on account of a letter
> from President Polk introducing him to Gen. Wool and
> saying he had resided in the country some time and
> might perhaps be of service to him in his operations.
> This makes him appear in their eyes something of a spy,
> though his intentions were of an entire different nature,

and his motives, his feelings to all parties of the purest kind. . . . Let us hope and pray, therefore, that our Almighty Father, The Just Judge, will be with him, and deliver him from the hands of his enemies.[12]

In early November, when Chihuahua officials learned of the advance of a force of Missouri volunteers under the command of Colonel Alexander Doniphan, they decided to make a stand north of El Paso del Norte. On 25 December a Mexican force under Captain Antonio Ponce de León's command met them at the Battle of Brazito, twenty-eight miles northwest of El Paso del Norte. In a clash lasting about thirty minutes, Doniphan's men routed the Mexican troops. Reportedly, the Mexicans misinterpreted a bugle call, leaving them in a confused, demoralized condition and at the mercy of a strong American charge. The Mexicans had the lone howitzer on the field that day, but Doniphan's men had the superior firepower.

Recent research on the site and significance of the Battle of Brazito indicates that the location was southwest of Vado Hill rather than to the northwest, as had been popularly supposed. Furthermore, the American triumph was of much greater significance than historians had earlier thought, since it secured New Mexico for the United States and established the basis for its legal claim to New Mexico.[13]

Doniphan's forces entered El Paso del Norte on 27 December and quickly arrested several Mexicans for anti-American activities. Among them were Prefect Bermúdez and the priest, Ramón Ortiz, who had been so hospitable toward the prisoners of the ill-fated Texan–Santa Fe Expedition of 1841.[14]

The United States Army remained in El Paso del Norte during January 1847 since Doniphan was not clear about his next assignment. His problems were immensely complicated with the arrival from Santa Fe of some 150 merchants and 315 wagons of merchandise valued at two thousand to three thousand dollars per wagon. Since the war was obviously interfering with sales and

profits, the merchants pressured Doniphan into providing a van-
guard and sufficient protection to ensure that the goods could
eventually be sold rather than falling into the hands of the Mexican
army. At length, after concluding that General John Wool's army
in Coahuila, for reasons unknown, was not going to invade
Chihuahua, Doniphan, his army, and the merchants, with Father
Ortiz as hostage, departed for the state capital on 8 February 1847.
A few days later Doniphan organized the merchants into two
infantry companies called the Traders Battalion, hoping that they
might become a military asset instead of a liability. On 28 February
Doniphan's army defeated a Mexican force at the Battle of
Sacramento and entered Chihuahua two days later. Although most
Anglo-American merchants who had been held were released,
James Magoffin was sent to Durango under heavy guard.[15]

While imprisoned in Chihuahua from September 1846 to
March 1847, Magoffin was scheduled to go on trial for espionage.
Mexican officials had captured a letter from General Kearny that
described in great detail Magoffin's role in the occupation of New
Mexico, and this evidence constituted a veritable death warrant.
Fortunately for Magoffin, his prestige in Chihuahua; a well-placed
bribe of 3,392 bottles of champagne; and the possibility that Father
Ortiz, being held hostage by the Americans, might be shot, secured
the disappearance of the incriminating document, and the case
was dropped. As Magoffin later reported, the military judge con-
fronted him with the Kearny letter before the other authorities had
seen it. "We understood one another; he told me to tear it up,
which I did in his presence, for I was a prisoner and it was not safe
for either of us that I should keep it. That affair cost me $3,800,
and deprived me of General Kearny's statement to lay before the
Government." Although never tried for espionage, Magoffin was
held as an enemy alien until his release in June 1847, nine months
by his own reckoning.[16]

Following his liberation Magoffin journeyed to Missouri,
Kentucky, and on to Washington, D.C., to present his claim for services rendered during the war. The itemized statement he

submitted totaled $37,780.96, but he met unexpected resistance in Washington. The secretary of war, George W. Crawford, contended that Magoffin had never had a contract with Secretary Marcy and the United States government was therefore not obliged to pay. Magoffin framed the following reply on 4 April 1849:

> Hon. Mr. Crawford
> Secretary of War
> Sir:
> The remark which you made that Mr. Marcy said there was no contract with me for my services in Mexico & the time that has elapsed since, without hearing anything, naturally makes me uneasy, & I write this brief statement for the purpose of showing my views of my case. I certainly made no contract with the Government nor did such an idea enter into my head. I engaged, at the request of President Polk, to go to Mexico, where I had been for many years, to be of service to our troops; & I took what they gave me, to wit, letters to accredit me to the General; they did accredit me and employ me. I went into Santa Fe ahead of Genl Kearny & smoothed the way for his bloodless conquest of New Mexico. Col. Archuleta would have fought. I quieted him. It was he who afterwards made the revolt which was put down with much bloodshed by Genl Price. Fight was in him, and it would have come out at first, carrying Armijo with him if it had not been for my exertions. I recommended to Genl Kearny to give him some place, which would compromise him, which the General intended to do, but was prevented by some cause to me unknown, and the consequence was the revolt at Taos, the death of Governor Bent, & all the bloodshed that took place. Archuleta fled to the South and did not return till after the peace. He was second in command & had about a thousand of the best troops in

New Mexico, and if he had held out for resistance, Armijo would have been obliged to have done the same, and a bloody resistance would have been made in the defiles through which Genl Kearny had to pass. Bloodless possession of New Mexico was what President Polk wished; it was obtained through my means. I could state exactly how I drew Archuleta from his intention to fight. The papers which I filed, Dr. Connelly's letter, Major Cooke's and Capt. Turner's, all allude to it, and Genl Kearny's was explicit. After this service, I went forward under the directions of Genl Kearny to render the same service to Genl Wool. I entered Chihuahua. He did not arrive; & that led to my imprisonment, to the great loss of my property, & the vast expenses which I had to incur. It was to smooth the way for Genl Wool that I went to Chihuahua. If he had come I should probably have done as much for him as I did for Genl Kearny. I have neglected my business for near three years, have not been with my family during that time, have made great expenses, and suffered great losses; and the statement of items which I presented is not an account, but a statement to give some idea of what it would take to remunerate me. The service I rendered is above payment. I was engaged in June 1846 by the President & Secretary of War, in the presence & with the knowledge of Senator Benton; the service and engagement was acknowledged by President Polk, after I got back, in the presence of Senator Atchison, and the only reason for not paying me was the want of money. . . . Senator Atchison has gone away; Senator Benton is going and I begin to feel uneasy about my compensation and beg your attention to my case.
Yours Respectfully,
J. W. Magoffin[17]

Magoffin's efforts finally brought results. Congress appropriated fifty thousand dollars "for the use of the army, with the understanding that all, or a substantial part of the money would be used to pay Magoffin's claim." He finally agreed to accept forty thousand dollars, but Secretary Crawford countered with an offer of thirty thousand dollars that Magoffin reluctantly accepted.[18]

Thinking to renew the Chihuahua trade, he returned to Independence, Missouri, where he organized a wagon train. When he arrived in El Paso del Norte in April 1849, however, he found that the high customs duties destroyed any hope of a profit from sales. He then settled down on the northeast bank of the Rio Grande, now a part of the United States, and laid the cornerstone of Magoffinsville, destined to play a role of great significance in the history of El Paso, Texas.[19]

Chapter Five

MAGOFFINSVILLE, 1849–1857

Momentous changes took place in the El Paso area after 1848, the year the Treaty of Guadalupe Hidalgo established the Rio Grande as an international boundary between the United States and Mexico. Before that date there were six settlements in a chain along the right bank of the Rio Grande: El Paso del Norte, Real de San Lorenzo, Senecú, and the three downriver towns of Ysleta, Socorro, and San Elizario, located on what amounted to an island created by the shifting river in the 1830s. In 1848, however, El Paso del Norte became a border town, and within a year Anglo-Americans had established five settlements north of the river. They were soon joined by the three Mexican towns of Ysleta, Socorro, and San Elizario after American officials ruled, in spite of Mexican protests, that they were on the American side. Since 1848, therefore, the El Paso area has been the product of two cultural traditions—the Spanish-Mexican North, and the Anglo-American Southwest.[1]

The first and northernmost of the five settlements the Anglo-Americans founded was Frontera, which T. Frank White established as a trading post about eight miles above El Paso del Norte. Since his hopes that a military post would be erected at Frontera never materialized, White rented his property to the United States boundary commissioner, John Russell Bartlett, who built an observatory there. To the south of Frontera and across from El Paso del Norte, Mexican War veteran Simeon Hart late in 1849 established his flour mill known as El Molino. Several years later he built his residence, now La Hacienda Cafe. To the east of Hart's mill lay the property of Benjamin Franklin Coons, who purchased it from *paseño* aristocrat Juan María Ponce de León. To the east of Coons's Ranch, or Franklin, as it came to be called, was the future site of Magoffinsville, which soon became the largest and most important of the El Paso settlements. Finally, to the east of the Magoffinsville site was the property of Hugh Stephenson, well-known merchant of El Paso del Norte. He had married Juana Ascárate, daughter of a prominent landowning family of El Paso del Norte, and they established a settlement on that part of the family estate the shifting Rio Grande had placed on the United States side. In time it came to be known as Concordia.[2]

By 1849 there were compelling reasons for establishing a military post in the area, including defense of the new boundary, protection of the new settlements against Apache attacks, and maintenance of law and order, which had already become critical with the arrival of hordes of California emigrants. A recommendation of Secretary of War Marcy in July 1848 that a post ought to be established on the north side of the Rio Grande opposite El Paso del Norte was implemented when six companies of infantry from San Antonio reached the area on 8 September 1849 under the command of Major Jefferson Van Horne. Two companies were stationed at the old presidio of San Elizario, while the other four established quarters across the river from El Paso del Norte on Benjamin F. Coons's ranch, which Van Horne named the Post Opposite El Paso, New Mexico.[3]

Major Van Horne regarded this site as temporary, and since Coons was charging the army $350 per month for rent, he favored San Elizario as the best location for the permanent post. The merchants in the area were strongly opposed, however. Under James W. Magoffin's leadership, they drew up a petition pointing out that any removal of troops from the Post Opposite El Paso would leave the major routes through the Pass of the North unprotected, exposing United States citizens to Indian depredations and endangering property valued at three hundred thousand dollars. Law and order would break down, the merchants argued, and the large number of outlaws infesting the town of El Paso del Norte would soon victimize the area. For the time being the army retained four infantry companies on Benjamin F. Coons's property, leaving the other two in San Elizario. As it turned out, however, the victory of the merchants was short-lived.[4]

In June 1849 Magoffin laid the foundations of Magoffinsville, the midpoint between Santa Fe and Chihuahua, on unclaimed land east of Coons's Ranch. Starting with a grist mill powered by water from an extension of the *acequia madre* built by Juan María Ponce de León of El Paso del Norte, Magoffin added a plaza surrounded by eight stores and warehouses for the merchandise his wagon trains supplied from San Antonio. His mule farm helped hundreds of California emigrants replenish their worn-out stock. Then came the completion of a magnificent mansion of hacienda proportions with a garden where he frequently hosted army officers and government officials in the grand manner. With "delicacies prepared in New York and Paris for the foreign market," wrote Paul Horgan, he could serve a "cold collation . . . that would have done credit to the caterer of a metropolitan hotel." While Bartlett, the United States boundary commissioner, was staying at Magoffinsville for a time, he gave a party there that lasted all night. "It was a success," Horgan added, "even to four great 'new-fashioned chandeliers improvised for the occasion' out of sardine tins fixed to a hoop off a pork barrel, wrapped with Apache calicoes and supplied with a 'dozen burners each,' that 'shed such a ray of light upon the festal hall, as rendered the charms of the fair señoritas doubly captivating.'" In Bartlett's opinion Magoffinsville was "the American El Paso," and he predicted that it would remain the center of American settlements in the El Paso area.[5]

For more than a decade and a half James Magoffin was the

most powerful and influential individual in the El Paso area; his leadership and the respect he commanded were unquestioned and unchallenged during the Magoffinsville years. A man of distinguished presence, urbane, lively, energetic, and fearless, Magoffin was always the genial host, naturally convivial, full of Irish wit, master storyteller, and dispenser of fine wine and champagne. Fluent in both languages of the El Paso area, Don Santiago was admired by Americans and Mexicans alike during his entire adult life, whether in Matamoros, Chihuahua, or El Paso. Sharing the widely known hospitality of the Magoffin household was his first wife's younger sister, Dolores Valdez, or Lolita, whom he married on 17 August 1850 in a ceremony performed by the chief justice of the county, Charles Hoppin. The children, all born in Chihuahua to Magoffin's first wife, were Samuel, Joseph, Josephine, Ursula, Annetta, and Angela. A seventh child, Gertrudis, died at an early age.[6]

George Wythe Baylor, Magoffin's good friend, told the following story about a trip Magoffin made in the early 1850s to Las Cruces.

> Among the many events of his life in the early days of El Paso, he went up to Las Cruces in all the style and grandeur then in vogue, having an ambulance, four fine mules, outriders, etc. When they reached the usual place to noon, which was chosen because it was open to the Rio Grande and afforded no chance for the Apaches to ambuscade them when they went down the bank to water their stock, they never looked in the scrubby chaparral brush back from the camping grounds. All went down with the stock to guard it from possible stampede and after filling their canteens, washing their faces, and letting their animals drink their fill, they started up the bank with Don Santiago ahead. But as soon as his head got on a level with the bank a sight met his astonished optics that made him drop out of sight quickly. About 25 Apaches had taken possession of his

ambulance and were helping themselves to everything portable—harness, blankets, grub, and among other things, a stove-pipe beaver hat which the judge carried to impress the natives. There was nothing to do but watch them, as they were too numerous to be attacked. So they stood ready to repel any attack and trusted the Apaches would leave as soon as they looted the camp. The Indians soon had out the judge's brown jug and emptied it. On further search they brought out a basket of the best brand of champagne from under the seat. This discovery brought from them a whoop of joy, the brown jug having already made them hilarious. They had out several bottles and went to work industriously to get out the corks. As it was hot, and the champagne well shaken up, it was naturally in a very highly explosive condition. The first one who got the wire cut and the cork nearly out must have had it pointed at the face of the chief, for it went off with the report of a pocket pistol, taking that worthy in the eye. One of the Indians had on the beaver and another had on the old-fashioned leather box in which it was kept, such as you never see nowadays. That one shot settled the fight. The Apaches tumbled over each other in their terror and dropped everything, stampeding like a herd of mustangs. The judge and his men then rushed to the ambulance and recovered all their property, the Indians never making a halt as far as they could see them on their way to the Organ Mountains.[7]

The basis of Magoffin's extensive operations in the early 1850s was his merchandising and livestock activities, supplemented by income from a ranch known as Canutillo, located about fifteen miles to the north. In addition, he furnished Bartlett's boundary commission with food, clothing, and supplies for a sum totaling more than fifty-five hundred dollars and sold livestock and merchandise to the hundreds of travelers passing through. By this time he had established the framework for his business partnership with the wealthy and influential José Cordero of Chihuahua, which in time became the largest, most important commercial operation in the American Southwest.[8]

Not all was profit, however, for Magoffin suffered great live-stock losses because of terrifying Indian raids between 1851 and 1853. Just as the settlers had predicted, the removal of troops from the El Paso area in September 1851 left the frontier completely exposed to raiding Apaches who murdered and plundered at will. In his letter of 5 August 1852 to the local Committee of El Paso County, Magoffin reported:

> Since 1 January I have lost 60 mules taken within 150 yards of my house, the first lot in the direction of the copper mines, and the second taken to the Sacramento mountain. About the 1st of March they took from the Canutillo Ranch 15 miles from El Paso and 30 miles from Fort Fillmore on the main road to Santa Fe all my stock of cattle, killing one man and taking off a boy, say 16 years old. On the 25th of July they made a 2nd attack on my Ranch about 10 a. m. taking all the outfit I had there for farming purposes—Cows, Calves, the Indians about 60 in number. I have since that time received no further damage from them but daily I hear of their terrible outrages committed upon citizens on both sides of the river.[9]

The deplorable conditions, as the committee reported in a petition to the governor, had resulted in the flight of hundreds of Mexican families across the river to Mexico, where they sought refuge, safety, and the establishment of the new towns of Guadalupe Bravos and San Ignacio. Many respectable citizens of Mexico, said the petition, had accepted American citizenship and made the county of El Paso their place of residence, but they had subsequently been forced to sacrifice their property and compelled to leave the country.[10]

At length, District Judge Joel L. Ankrim wrote the military authorities and listed the losses suffered during the past two years: twenty-three Indian attacks had resulted in the loss of lives and property, disruption of business, and a general feeling of insecurity. This information was then enclosed in a report submitted by Colonel Joseph K. F. Mansfield. He had previously inspected western military posts and recommended that one be located opposite the town of El Paso del Norte, either at Magoffinsville or at Smith's Ranch, preferably the former. The result was the post established at Magoffinsville in January 1854, with four companies under Major Edmund B. Alexander's command being assigned quarters in buildings James Magoffin owned. In March the new post was officially designated Fort Bliss in honor of Major William W. S. Bliss, chief of staff for Zachary Taylor during the war with Mexico and later his son-in-law.[11]

The most serious reversal Magoffin experienced in his business ventures arose from a tax he levied on salt deposits located on the eastern slopes of the San Andres Mountains in New Mexico. His action was a clear violation of traditional frontier policy that common salt, regarded as a vital necessity, was reserved without restriction for the general public's benefit and thus exempt from levies a private owner might impose. After acquiring an interest in a tract that was in an area noted for its salt springs, Magoffin in 1853 levied a toll on all who took the precious commodity from the springs. Sensing the mounting opposition to his actions and then discovering that a train of carts was about to leave Doña Ana County, New Mexico, to obtain salt at the springs, Magoffin took immediate steps to ensure that the levy was paid. He enlisted the services of William Ford, sheriff of El Paso County, who organized a posse of twenty-eight men armed with a howitzer.[12]

On a cold January morning in 1854, the posse lay in wait for the *salineros*, who had learned of Magoffin's plan to enforce the levy. One hundred twenty-five New Mexicans with twenty-six carretas met the posse head on, and the two groups then entered into a parley. Sheriff Ford served his papers on the men of Mesilla, who refused to accede to Magoffin's demands. After a wild flurry of rifle fire lasting ten minutes, several rounds from the howitzer drove off the salineros, who left their livestock to be captured by the posse and driven back to Texas.[13]

Magoffin's victory in the matter of enforcing payment proved to be temporary. He and several of his associates were indicted at Mesilla for armed conspiracy against the peace and dignity of the New Mexico Territory. The defendants, however, were beyond the jurisdiction of the territorial court, and the efforts of Governor David Meriwether of New Mexico to have them extradited proved unsuccessful. At length Magoffin, concerned about his damaged reputation, as well as the threat of criminal prosecution, agreed to surrender the captured animals to their rightful owners and make full restitution for all damages resulting from the skirmish with the salineros. "That Don Santiago and his associates got off as lightly as they did," noted Strickland, "argues that he had not lost his old magic in dealing with officialdom." Twenty-three years later a similar case in San Elizario known as the Salt War, which involved the same sacred public tradition, was not settled nearly as peacefully.[14]

The early 1850s saw the inauguration of mail service from San Antonio through El Paso to Santa Fe. A big, broad-shouldered frontiersman named Henry Skillman was the first to carry the mail. "He was over six feet high," wrote Nancy Lee Hammons, "with long yellow curls hanging down over the shoulders of his buckskin jacket. He carried pistols, two of them, and two bowie knives in his belt, and a Sharp's rifle back of the seat." He established a monthly passenger service using four-horse coaches. The fare from San Antonio to El Paso was $100; through fare to Santa Fe was $125. Joining Skillman as stage driver was the fabled William Alexander Wallace, named Bigfoot for his long-standing feud with a Lipan Apache who had left huge moccasin tracks in his path.[15]

The increased volume of mail brought the establishment of a post office for El Paso, Texas, in 1852, although the name Franklin continued to be used on both sides of the border for a number of years. In 1857 George E. Giddings initiated a semimonthly mail and passenger service between San Antonio and San Diego, California, often called the "Jackass Line" because of its use of mules over most of the route. Eighty-seven stage stations were erected for the service known as "the longest uninterrupted route in the United States if not in the world."[16]

Hammons also wrote of El Paso County's encounter with "one of the most unusual caravans ever seen in the United States . . . the first and only Camel Brigade ever organized" in this country. Twenty-five camels, each carrying a five-hundred-pound load, commanded by Lieutenant Edward F. Beale, arrived in San Elizario on the morning of 26 July 1857. According to Lieutenant Beale, the local Mexican-American population was very excited by the visit of the camels, so much so that they all accompanied the soldiers when they set up camp. The following evening Beale went to Franklin and then spent the next day at Fort Bliss. That night he "dined with Mr. McGoffin, and attended a pleasant party at his house afterwards."[17]

Fort Bliss was the favorite military post of army wives in the late 1850s. Lydia Spenser Lane was delighted when her husband received orders to report in May 1857.

> May 25 found us at the most delightful station we ever had—Fort Bliss—the old and first Fort Bliss, far more pleasant than those of the same name which have succeeded it, though the present post is more pretentious in every way. . . .
>
> The garrison at Fort Bliss was very small, but there were some very pleasant people (citizens) living at and not very far from the post. There was a good deal of social visiting among us all, and an occasional formal entertainment, to which everybody was invited.

While there she naturally had occasion to meet Magoffin and his family. She set down the following observations: "Colonel Magoffin, the sutler, had a large house, and several pretty, well-educated daughters. Mrs. Magoffin was a Spanish woman, from whom the daughters inherited much grace and beauty. Of course they were great belles, and their home was very attractive. . . ."[18]

Frederick Augustus Percy was responsible for the most impressive of the contemporary sketches of Fort Bliss. He did not exaggerate when he titled his work *Magnificent Sketch of Fort Bliss late Magoffinsville—Drawn, Designed, and Painted by The Ancient Briton, dated 31 May 1854*. It appeared in Percy's *El Sabio Sembrador*, and Rex Strickland edited and republished it in 1969 in *El Paso in 1854*. Book designer Carl Hertzog reproduced the drawing in color in exact facsimile. The view is to the west, with post buildings on the south and west sides of an open square. On the north is Magoffin's complex: sutler's stores, residence, and chapel. A similar depiction of Fort Bliss in 1855, though not as magnificent as Percy's, may be found in W. W. H. Davis's *El Gringo*.[19]

Chapter Six

THE MAGOFFIN-CORDERO PARTNERSHIP, 1849–1857

In the 1850s Magoffinsville became the headquarters of the largest, most important commercial operation in the American Southwest. It specialized in European cotton goods and fabrics that Magoffin imported through the firm of Peter Harmony Nephews and Company of New York City. From New York the merchandise was shipped by rail to Pittsburgh, then by riverboat to St. Louis and Independence, Missouri. From there it went by mule train to Santa Fe, then south down the historic Camino Real to the customhouse at El Paso del Norte and on to Chihuahua. Brother Samuel handled sales in Santa Fe, and Magoffin's partner, the wealthy, influential José Cordero, supervised activities in Chihuahua and contributed to the operation as needed. Magoffin used part of the thirty thousand dollars he received from the United States government to get the partnership started.[1]

Born in Valle de Allende on 27 December 1798, José Cordero had already become a highly successful merchant when Magoffin met him on his visit to Chihuahua in 1832. By the 1840s Cordero was reportedly the richest man in Chihuahua. He had also become involved in Chihuahua politics, serving in various state and local offices, and was one of the principal organizers of the Liberal party in Chihuahua in 1845. Along the way, he had contributed large sums of money to improve social and economic conditions in the state, fight Apaches and Comanches, and defend New Mexico against the Texans and the Mexican nation against the United States.[2]

Because of his political liberalism and friendship with American merchants, however, Cordero became increasingly unpopular in political circles. His chief enemy was Angel Trías, a staunch conservative who enjoyed the loyal support of Antonio López de Santa Anna. After organizing a movement to overthrow Trías in 1850, Cordero was elected to a four-year term as governor of Chihuahua in 1852. He served for less than a year, however, because his policies, according to Chihuahua historian Francisco Almada, alienated the Mexican Congress, the commandant general, and the minister of war. Santa Anna engineered a conservative revolt that returned Trías to the governorship.[3]

American merchants knew Cordero well, and on one occasion Santa Fe trader James Josiah Webb recalled that "there was a capitalist in Chihuahua who was always ready to avail himself of a bargain, with cash in hand for almost any amount. This was Don José Cordero." Webb recounted the story of an old trader who fancied himself the keenest in the business. One day Cordero made a generous offer, which the trader declined. After thinking it over for a few days, he decided to accept the original offer only to find that Cordero was then offering about a thousand dollars less, which the old trader also refused to accept. When he went to Cordero the following day to accept that offer, he was surprised to learn that the offer had been good only for a day and that the new offer was fifteen hundred dollars less than that of the day before. So it was that Cordero outsmarted the old trader to the tune of twenty-five hundred dollars.[4]

Boundary Commissioner John Russell Bartlett took note of the Magoffin-Cordero relationship when he visited Chihuahua in 1852. Bartlett commented on the extensive trade between Chihuahua and the United States by means of wagon trains, or caravans, from St. Louis, Missouri, and San Antonio, Texas. The usual route was by way of St. Louis; Santa Fe, New Mexico; and El Paso, Texas, over a distance of more than fifteen hundred miles, requiring several months for the trip. José Cordero, governor of Chihuahua at the time, was one of the principal merchants. Second to him were several highly regarded Anglo-American trading houses. Chihuahua boasted a number of well-stocked stores where every kind of merchandise could be had.

Bartlett explained what a merchant involved in the Chihuahua trade could expect to undergo if he hoped to succeed.

> If a merchant here desires to make his purchases himself in New York or our other great markets, he must leave here in the fall, when it will require from forty to fifty days to reach his destination, by way of New Orleans. His goods must then be purchased and shipped either to Indianola, on the Gulf of Mexico, to be sent by San Antonio, or to St. Louis, Missouri, and thence by water to Independence. . . . Wagons, mules, harness, and the various trappings must be purchased, and teamsters procured; all of which requires much time and a large outlay. The large Missouri wagons, which carry from five thousand to five thousand five hundred pounds, cost about two hundred dollars each; the best Kentucky mules, ninety to one hundred dollars; harness, one hundred dollars; water kegs, extra chains, ropes, etc., twenty-five dollars for each wagon. These large wagons require ten mules each; so a complete team ready for the plains would cost from twelve hundred to thirteen hundred dollars; and twenty of these, which is not a large train, twenty-six thousand dollars. Then each team must have its teamster at from twenty to twenty-five dollars a month; and a wagon-master or director of the train at from eighty to one hundred dollars a month. From fifteen to twenty extra mules would

be necessary for such a train; as, on their long journeys, accidents cannot be avoided. Men to herd and take care of the animals must also be provided; and, finally, provisions for the journey. . . . If the merchant gets back with his goods in ten months from the time he left, without encounters with hostile Indians, or the loss of any of his wagons and their contents, in fording streams and otherwise, he may consider himself fortunate. It cannot be expected that a merchant will be satisfied with very small profits after such an expedition.[5]

To get his partnership under way with Magoffin, José Cordero invested nineteen thousand pesos in August 1850 to cover existing obligations and informed Magoffin that he was considering running for governor. Magoffin appointed Tomás Zuloaga as his sales representative in Chihuahua. One of five sons of Carlos Zuloaga, a wealthy hacendado, the young Zuloaga's zeal and energy produced assets of more than seven thousand dollars by late 1852 and more than eighteen thousand dollars by late 1853. In early 1854 the New York importing firm of Harmony Nephews and Company notified Magoffin that the United States government had deposited twenty thousand dollars in his account. By that time, however, Zuloaga had left the partnership to join his good friend, Governor Angel Trías, in El Paso del Norte to assist in the defense of the Mesilla territory against New Mexico. The assets of the Magoffin-Cordero partnership were then more than forty thousand dollars.[6]

Replacing the capable Zuloaga was young Isaac Lightner, husband of Carmelita, who was the youngest sister of Magoffin's wife, Lolita. No sooner had he arrived in Chihuahua than he reported to Magoffin that merchandise valued at $18,000 had been seized for failure to pay sufficient duties and that Magoffin should file a claim for $48,000 to cover the loss of the merchandise and damages. He wrote that he was unsatisfied with the $10,500 José Cordero paid him for the damaged goods and was therefore asking Magoffin to contact the firm of Wood Bacon and Company to collect the remaining amount. Lightner stated that he would pay the firm one-third of the amount collected.[7]

Whether Magoffin took any action on Lightner's request is unknown. It seems unlikely, however, since subsequent correspondence indicates that relations between the two remained strained. In a letter to Magoffin of 18 April 1854 Lightner wrote: "I was sorry to see that in my attempt to please you with a frank and candid proceeding (as I am accustomed to do with all with whom I deal), it appears that it has caused you some uneasiness which I think is unnecessary and calculated to inconvenience me very much." Lightner's days in Chihuahua were numbered. He left six thousand dollars with Cordero, possibly in the hope that he would take some action to recover the lost merchandise.[8]

The most prominent Mexican enterprise in the copper-mining trade in the early nineteenth century belonged to the Elguea family of Chihuahua. A representative of the family had leased the Santa Rita mine to Esteban Curcier. Francisco Elguea, who owned mines in Parral, wrote Magoffin representing his family in June 1850, asking him to find a buyer for his family's copper operations. He fixed the sale price at forty thousand dollars, with Magoffin to receive 25 percent. Elguea reminded Magoffin that the copper business had enabled Curcier to amass a considerable fortune.[9]

Three years later, on 3 November 1853, Elguea wrote Magoffin again, stating that he had not received any word regarding the disposition of the mines. Another year went by, and Elguea wrote Magoffin a third time. He had learned that Curcier was now working as an agent for an English company interested in mines as an investment; Magoffin should contact him as soon as possible at his hacienda near Mápula. Nothing came of this. Magoffin, no doubt fully aware of the condition of the mines, could see no reason to become involved in their sale and had other pressing matters, such as the Chihuahua trade, claiming his attention.[10]

By March 1855 the Magoffin-Cordero partnership's assets had fallen to a thousand dollars, forcing Magoffin to return to Chihuahua while entrusting Magoffinsville affairs to his best friend, Josiah Fraser Crosby, a South Carolina lawyer who had come west for his health. Magoffin quickly restored the financial strength of the partnership and, with the help of forty-two hundred dollars in credit from the House of Harmony, increased its assets to more than fifteen thousand dollars by early 1856. By the end of the year, however, they had plummeted to five thousand dollars, and soon after he returned home in early 1857. The fatal blow came when the Harmony firm notified him that his funds were utterly depleted. In a letter to Cordero, Magoffin insisted that the United States government still owed him sixty-four hundred dollars. He assured his partner that if the money did not arrive shortly, he would return to Chihuahua and discuss all remaining financial problems following a trip to inspect the Santa Rita copper mine. It was unlikely that a continuation of the partnership would be seriously considered.[11]

Historians of the Chihuahua trade will be forever indebted to Cordero and his staff for compiling the financial records of the partnership from 1850 to 1857. Listed are the various personal accounts; the merchandise transactions; and the names of buyers, prices, dates, and methods of payment, whether by specie, bullion, bank draft, or promissory note. Each transaction was noted in one of two columns, *haber* (credit) or *debe* (debit), thus approximating a modern system of double-entry bookkeeping recording assets and liabilities. All in all, the records reveal in detail the day-to-day business activities of two great figures engaged in the Chihuahua trade in the mid-nineteenth century.[12]

In the years between 1858 and 1861, Mexico experienced a major political and socioeconomic revolution known as the War of the Reform. Under the leadership of Benito Juárez, a Zapotec Indian from Oaxaca, the Liberal party in Mexico proclaimed the Constitution of 1857. It called for the establishment of constitutional government; a federal republic; individual rights and guarantees; public education; the civil registration of births, marriages, and deaths; and the breaking of the political and economic power of the Catholic church in Mexico. When progressive and conservative forces could find no way to compromise on this program of nine-teenth-century liberalism, the result was a bloody, devastating civil war that paralyzed commercial activities throughout the entire nation.[13]

The ensuing chaos prevailing throughout Mexico permitted individual states, particularly those on the northern frontier, to do much as they pleased without fear of intervention by the central government. Thus, in 1858 Governor Ramón Guerra of Tamaulipas established a *zona libre* (free-trade zone) along the state's northeastern frontier that provided favorable trade privi-leges to the border towns on the south bank of the Rio Grande, including Matamoros, Reynosa, Camargo, Mier, Guerrero, and Nuevo Laredo. All foreign goods were allowed to enter this special trade zone duty-free, bringing prosperity to the state of Tamaulipas. During the American Civil War these towns erected free ports of entry for the Confederates to export their cotton, receiving in return large supplies of arms and munitions. Matamoros, where James Magoffin had made his first fortune thirty years before, became one of the largest ports in North America.[14]

In contrast to the prosperity prevailing in Matamoros was the situation in El Paso del Norte and the surrounding area. David Diffenderfer, a veteran of seven years' service as United States con-sul in El Paso del Norte, wrote in April 1858 that conditions in Mexico were deplorable. "Business is entirely prostrated," he wrote,

> the people are starving, robbing and thieving are the
> order of the day, taxes are enormous, and thus the
> thinking people of northern Mexico feel the necessity of
> doing something for themselves. Some favor an inde-
> pendent republic; others feel the need for a United
> States protectorate, and still others favor annexation to
> the United States. Should this happen the United States
> would have to maintain a considerable force to keep

order, and it will need to educate the coming genera-
tion. There is not an honest man in Mexico—people
take office only to enrich themselves.[15]

Magoffin agreed with the consul's assessment. In a letter of 24
May 1860 to Governor Sam Houston of Texas, he said he was in
full accord with the governor's suggestion that a United States pro-
tectorate should be established in Mexico. "That fine country,"
wrote Magoffin, "has totally gone to ruin for want of protection—
too bad, but so it is. I hope to see the day myself when Mexico will
be freed from oppression. Texas has to be the single best hope that
makes tyranny and oppression tremble throughout that noble
country."[16]

By 1860 the civil strife in Mexico was entering its third year.
Trade had come to a standstill, and the country was paralyzed.
Cordero decided to move his family to the United States and in
February brought his wife and two children to the El Paso area. He
settled them at La Cuadrilla, a small village east of San Elizario,
and as a result, he and his family were included in the United States
census of 1860. He was listed as a merchant, age fifty-three, with
an estate valued at $250,000. His wife, Carmela, was thirty-eight,
and her property was said to be worth $5,000. There were two
children: Josefa, thirteen, and Pablo, eleven. The census listed
Magoffin as a post sutler, age fifty-nine, with assets of $100,000.
His family included his wife, Dolores, thirty-five, and their four
children: Ursulita, twenty-two; Annetta, nineteen; Samuel, twenty-
five; and Joseph, twenty-three. Samuel was listed as a wagon master and Joseph as a clerk.[17]

By August 1860 the tide had turned in Mexico in favor of the
Liberal cause, and under Benito Juárez's leadership, Liberal forces
entered Mexico City on New Year's Day 1861. The rejoicing
throughout the war-torn nation was short-lived, however, as the
new regime soon faced yet another national crisis, a French military intervention sponsored by Emperor Napoleon III. Although

this was a clear violation of the Monroe Doctrine, the United States, involved in its own Civil War, had to delay effective enforcement for four years. Mexican resistance to the European enemy was largely limited to one supreme effort at Puebla on 5 May 1862, the Cinco de Mayo, a day destined to become one of Mexico's greatest national celebrations.[18]

Chapter Seven

THE DREAM OF A TRANSCONTINENTAL RAILROAD

I n the decade following the close of the war with Mexico, the United States government inaugurated and conducted an extensive program of exploration in west Texas, one phase of a general policy of developing the entire trans-Mississippi territory in the interest of the immigrant, the settler, the soldier, and the merchant. Captain Samuel G. French, assistant quartermaster of the expedition under the command of Major Jefferson Van Horne, noted in September 1849 "that El Paso, from its geographical position [at the thirty-second parallel], presents itself as a resting place on one of the great overland routes between the seaports of the Atlantic on one side and those of the Pacific on the other."[1]

In that same year another party under the command of Captain Randolph B. Marcy traveled from Fort Smith, Arkansas, to Santa Fe, then down the Rio Grande to Doña Ana or El Paso. Marcy reported that "there are probably as few difficulties to encounter as upon any other road that can be found in our country. . . . For a great portion of the distance, the surface of the earth is so perfectly firm and smooth that it would appear to have been designed by the Great Architect of the Universe for a railroad."[2]

Possibly the most enthusiastic champion of the thirty-second parallel as the best one for the construction of a transcontinental railroad was Captain John Pope. In early 1854 he conducted the most comprehensive survey yet undertaken of that latitude from the Rio Grande east to the Red River. Specifically, with regard to the El Paso area, he listed the settlements along the river: Molino, located below the abandoned ranch of Frontera at the rapids of the Rio Grande and about two miles upriver from El Paso [del Norte], and Franklin, about two miles downriver. At the time, four companies of the United States Eighth Infantry occupied the latter town, which was "almost entirely the property of Mr. James McGoffin, a wealthy and enterprising citizen of El Paso county."[3]

Thoroughly convinced of the importance of the railroad in the El Paso area's future, Magoffin became actively engaged in organizing community and state backing for a transcontinental railroad along the southern route through El Paso. The Texas legislature had already granted liberal charters to companies willing to build from the state's eastern border to the mountain gap in west Texas. Generous land grants came with every mile of track to be laid. Under the leadership of Senator Thomas Rusk of Texas, supporters of the project approached the directors of the Atlantic and Pacific Railroad Company to secure their involvement. Then they organized a personal trip to El Paso over the route the future railroad would most likely follow. They were treated to the hospitality of Magoffinsville where they met with local citizens and potential investors from Mexico. "Over glasses of the potent Pass brandy," wrote Wayne Austerman, "they planned the spanning of the continent and forged the linchpin that would bind El Paso to a trail of riches from the Gulf to the Pacific."[4]

The Treaty of Guadalupe Hidalgo, signed in 1848, raised several points that the international boundary compromise forged by John Russell Bartlett and his Mexican counterpart, General Pedro García Conde, failed to resolve. Three such issues, the status of the Santa Rita copper mine, a highly desirable transcontinental railroad site, and the fertile Mesilla Valley (some six thousand square

miles in extent), became objects of bitter dispute between New
Mexico and Chihuahua in 1853. Governor Angel Trías of
Chihuahua, who had fought the United States in the recent war,
challenged Governor William Carr Lane's claim of the area for
New Mexico by ordering his troops into the Mesilla Valley.
Governor Lane responded with a threat of similar action, but his
commander at Fort Fillmore refused to cooperate. James Magoffin
explained the situation to Bartlett in a letter.

> Governor Carr Lane of New Mexico paid us a visit a
> few weeks since and issued a proclamation to the
> authorities of El Paso del Norte that he intended to take
> possession of Mesilla, which created great excitement
> throughout the territory and in fact as far as the City of
> Mexico. General Trillas arrived here today with 750 sol-
> diers in order to defend the soil, but the Governor had
> returned home, not being supported by the citizens and
> getting no military aid, and so this matter rests. General
> Trillas will no doubt make his headquarters at El Paso
> del Norte for some time.[5]

With relations between the United States and Mexico near
rupture, the Franklin Pierce administration replaced Governor
Lane with David W. Meriwether. The new governor was to pursue
a negotiated resolution and "abstain from taking forcible possession
of the tract." President Pierce appointed as his minister to Mexico
James Gadsden, a South Carolina railroad executive and backer of
a southern transcontinental route to the Pacific. Arriving in Mexico,
Gadsden found Antonio López de Santa Anna's dictatorial regime
on the verge of bankruptcy and in desperate need of capital. On 30
December 1853 Santa Anna agreed to a treaty, usually called the
Gadsden Purchase Treaty, that permitted the United States to purchase, for fifteen million dollars, 29,760 square miles of territory
south of the Gila River, including the railroad route and the Mesilla
Valley. After several months of debate in both the House of

Representatives and the Senate that reduced the territory by 9,000 square miles and the purchase price to ten million dollars, the Senate ratified the treaty on 25 April 1854. From that time on, Southern interest in a transcontinental railroad remained high.[6]

Sensing the sudden importance of the Santa Rita copper mine, given its proximity to the railroad route, Magoffin wrote his brother Samuel to suggest how Francisco Elguea, the mine's owner, might be approached. Samuel replied on 24 August 1854.

> With regard to the copper mine in question, the time has now arrived when that matter should be promptly attended to. Harrison and myself will be able to impose on them in the way you propose in your letter to us in a most satisfactory manner, that is, to men of great wealth and influence, men that will give character to the property, and who have the perseverance and energy not to be stopped by any small obstacle that may present itself, men that will not stop if they take holt of this thing until they present it before the world in its true shape and worth, and in the most advantageous manner possible, and in all probability make millions out of it.

Samuel proceeded to give his brother James specific instructions.

> Now what we wish you to do is this—first say to Don Ignacio Ilgue that you have sold the property (positively) in question through your agent at St. Louis, Mo., then inform yourself of every particular with regard to the soundness of the title and certainly learn whether the title of the present owner has not been forfeited by noncompliance with the Spanish or Mexican laws with regard to entering and working mines etc. It will be necessary no doubt for you to employ someone who is *truthful* and conversant with the Spanish and Mexican

laws to look into this matter and give us a true statement of it. It must be done quickly and with the least
possible delay, as the parties here want to know in order
to shape their future action. The papers with the Plate
of copper are in possession of, but have not as yet been
able to have the papers translated to our satisfaction.
The Plate we have sent to N.Y. in order to ascertain its
worth and exact qualities. For particular instructions
and advice I refer you to the title of our old friend
Harrison under this same date. Hoping you may act
with the greatest promptness and let us hear from you
at least once a month until this matter is brought to a
conclusion. I remain your Brother S. Magoffin. P.S. Any
expense you may have in ascertaining the soundness of
title will of course be paid by the sellers of the property
as 'tis their business. Neither can they expect any pay
until the matter of title is made satisfactory.[7]

If Magoffin received his brother's letter of 24 August 1854, he
did not bother to answer. Pressing financial problems in the partnership with Cordero prompted Magoffin's departure in early
April 1855 for Chihuahua, where he remained for the rest of the
year. Receiving no word from his older brother, Samuel wrote to
him on 8 April 1855, posing the question:

What has become of the Santa Rita copper mine
papers and Plate? Harrison and I are both becoming
somewhat impatient as that mine, in case the Pacific
railroad plans have merit, must be worth the biggest
kind of a fortune. The road will be made no doubt, and
that before a great while, and must pass somewhere
convenient to it. Waste no time and send the papers in a
proper shape and legal form. Let them come with all
power placed in the hands of Harrison and myself.
There will be no difficulty in disposing of the property

if the papers come right. Let me hear from you on this subject immediately after you have seen this. I remain you brother S. Magoffin.[8]

Once again, if Magoffin received this letter of 8 April 1855, he never took the time to reply. As if this were not enough to upset Samuel, later that same year he suffered the loss of his beloved Susan, who died shortly after the birth of their fourth child, a daughter. "You no doubt have heard of the death of my wife," he wrote to Isaac Lightner on 15 December 1855. "I will not attempt to describe to you the sadness of my heart which this great affliction has caused."[9]

In 1856 the Andrew B. Gray Report of a survey of a route along the thirty-second parallel was published, with the approval of Jefferson Davis (secretary of war in the Pierce administration) and submitted to the Texas Western Railroad Company. Its estimated cost for constructing a railway from the eastern boundary of Texas to El Paso, a total of 783 miles, was $19,688,366, or an average cost per mile of $25,144. The railway, according to the report, would link the eastern and western limits of Texas and could be built in fewer than five years. It would thus provide service to towns and settlements such as San Elizario, Ysleta, Socorro, Magoffinsville, Franklin, Hart's Mill, Frontera, Fort Fillmore, Las Cruces, Doña Ana, and the villages of the Mesilla Valley. The state of Texas would cover construction costs, providing $7.50 an acre for the first 400 miles and $3.00 an acre for the remaining 383. Overall, the state of Texas would make available $44,789,760 for construction from the Mississippi River to the Pacific coast, twice the amount necessary to finance the entire Texas project. By 1856 it seemed the unification of the El Paso area and the rest of the state of Texas would soon become a reality.[10]

By early 1857 a transcontinental railroad at the thirty-second parallel had become the foremost demand of the El Paso leadership. On 4 April 1857 an article in the *Texas State Gazette* entitled "Democracy of El Paso" reported on a meeting in San Elizario that

Archibald C. Hyde, James Magoffin, Henry L. Dexter, John L. McCarty, and Judge Josiah Crosby attended. The proposals they offered reflected the west Texas cause by affirming their support for the primary concerns and policies of the Southern states, demanding sufficient military forces to protect the frontier settlers from hostile Indians, and urging the establishment of improved communications with the Mississippi Valley and California by means of stage routes and railroads.[11]

Captain John Pope's endorsement of the thirty-second parallel as suitable for a transcontinental railroad route greatly interested Southerners such as John C. Reid of Selma, Alabama, who visited the El Paso area in late 1857. He was impressed with the productivity of the valleys; of the Lower Valley settlements he liked San Elizario best. He preferred Magoffinsville to Stephenson's Ranch and thought that the facilities and strong adobe structures at Fort Bliss displayed good planning. He admired the prosperity of the town of Franklin, with its half-dozen dry-goods stores, custom-house, and post office. While there was much in El Paso del Norte that appealed to Reid—the fandangos, the fiesta of Our Lady of Guadalupe, the friendliness of the people, and the beautiful ladies—there was much he found distasteful—poverty, peonage, deteriorated buildings, the tariff, beggars, and thieves. On the whole, however, he could appreciate the area's potential and remained fully convinced that the thirty-second parallel offered advantages for a railroad that far exceeded all other routes.[12] Back in Selma by the following year, he published an account of his travels entitled *Reid's Tramp*. In his book, Reid predicted that El Paso, occupying the midpoint on the transcontinental railroad, would become the "most important inland city in America."[13]

Whether Magoffin ever received a copy of *Reid's Tramp* is unknown, but certainly from Reid's visit to Magoffinsville he concluded that he could count on the support of the Old South to fulfill his railroad dream. From that time forward, his uncompromising support of the South's policies could be expected whenever he felt its interests, particularly those relating to El Paso, were involved.

In September 1858 a new transportation service was completed between St. Louis and San Francisco that had a far greater impact on the El Paso area than any other until the arrival of the railroad. This was John Butterfield's Overland Mail, which traversed by stage the twenty-seven hundred miles from Tipton, Missouri, to San Francisco in twenty-five days. On 8 May 1858 Anson Mills arrived in El Paso. That September Mills was the architect and builder of the Butterfield station, the largest and best-equipped on the Butterfield route. Occupying half a city block, it was the most imposing structure in El Paso. Nearby was Ben Dowell's store, housing the post office and bar, which was the favorite meeting place in town. With the arrival of the railroad, its facilities would welcome visitors and handle freight, reminding everyone that El Paso had become a major continental crossroads. "If the proposed Atlantic and Pacific railroad should be constructed through Texas," noted W. W. H. Davis, "El Paso will be an important point on the route, and it will be the means of settling this whole valley with an enterprising population."[14]

El Paso had prospered and grown during the 1850s. El Paso County had been organized, the economy was healthy, and the population had topped four hundred. Moreover, there was the promise of the arrival of the railroad, and the community had already emerged as a vital way station on the southern route to California. As the new decade opened, the future looked bright. The Civil War and Reconstruction, however, caused growth and development to stagnate for more than a decade, dooming a number of the anticipated advances. Many El Pasoans doubtless shared the sentiment W. W. Mills expressed in *Forty Years in El Paso*: "Many a still, lonesome night have I listened to the roaring of the waters over the dam at Hart's Mill, a mile above the village, and tried to fancy it the rumbling of railroad trains, which were then fifteen hundred miles away. . . . I felt sure that the first road to the Pacific would pass through El Paso, and *so it would*, had it not been for the Rebellion."[15]

Chapter Eight

THE CONFEDERATE CAUSE: TRIUMPH AND TRAGEDY

The triumph of Abraham Lincoln in the 1860 election brought to the White House the candidate of the Republican Party, which adamantly opposed extending slavery into the territories of the United States. The response from the Southern states, including Texas, was immediate. Seven Southern states held conventions that adopted ordinances of secession from the Union even before Lincoln's inaugural on 4 March 1861. Meeting in Austin on 1 February 1861, the Texas state convention voted in favor of secession. The Mexican-American population of El Paso, which was far and away the majority, evinced little interest. Anglo-Americans, however, were almost all pro-Southern. While some owned slaves, notably Simeon Hart, the reason for the pro-Southern attitude had more to do with the fact that Jefferson Davis, the president of the Confederate States of America, had long been identified with the southern transcontinental railroad route, a cause dear to those with an investment in the future of El Paso.[1]

When word of the state convention made it to El Paso, a local election was held on the question of Texas's secession. Balloting took place in Ben Dowell's saloon, and only the Mills brothers, Anson and W. W., voted against leaving the Union. Although some nine hundred votes were counted, several hundred of which were cast by Mexican nationals from neighboring El Paso del Norte, such influential pro-Southerners as Simeon Hart, James Magoffin, and Josiah Crosby carried the day.[2]

When Texas seceded from the Union, General David E. Twiggs, the departmental commander, surrendered all military property to the commissioners of the state and ordered all United States troops to leave. In compliance with these instructions, Lieutenant Colonel I. V. D. Reeve, commandant of Fort Bliss, departed with his forces on 31 March 1861. Before abandoning his post, he turned over all military property, an estimated twelve-months' supply of subsistence and ammunition for two companies, to James Magoffin and Simeon Hart, the authorized Confederate agents for the area.[3]

On 28 April Magoffin wrote Governor Edward Clark to report that the commanding officer of Fort Bliss had informed him that there was not fifty cents' worth of property to be surrendered, but that his son (probably Samuel) had found property worth five thousand to eight thousand dollars at Fort Quitman, eighty miles downriver. Magoffin then revealed that a plot had been laid to rob Fort Quitman as soon as the troops left and that some Americans and foreigners had hired carts from the Mexicans to freight the property to the Mexican side of the border. He added that he had secured the names of "the rascals" in time and recovered about two-thirds of the property. His earnest wish now was to send the thieves to the penitentiary since the post was more exposed than any other, with bad men in the state of Chihuahua, miners in New Mexico, and Indians, and he hoped that a respectable force would soon be sent to maintain order. The leader of the robbery, he presumed, was a black Republican who was willing to risk everything for the loot.[4]

By early May 1861 the situation at Fort Bliss was desperate, as Josiah Crosby indicated in a letter of 9 May to Governor Clark. He proposed raising as many troops as possible and stationing them at Fort Bliss forthwith. Magoffin, who owned the fort and public property under state authority, would see to the rationing and arming of the new force. Crosby cautioned that this measure would provide no permanent solution, since these men, who were not properly mustered into military service, could come and go as they pleased. He asked the governor to provide for the El Paso area and issued a warning. "The loss of the public property at Bliss would prove a calamity. We shall endeavor to defend it as long as possible, and if reduced to the necessity, could destroy it."[5]

On 24 May Brigadier General Earl Van Dorn, Confederate commander of the Department of Texas, ordered the regarrisoning of the abandoned posts. Four companies and a battery of artillery were assigned to Fort Bliss, but these detachments of the Second Regiment Texas Mounted Rifles only reached their destination in late June. Command of these troops reoccupying Fort Bliss was entrusted to Lieutenant Colonel John R. Baylor, a daring and dashing Texan. Late in July Baylor and three hundred men advanced northward, occupied the Mesilla Valley, and forced the surrender of Colonel Isaac Lynde and seven hundred men at Fort Fillmore, thus clearing southern New Mexico and west Texas of Union forces. Since the provisions Hart and Magoffin supplied had played a most significant role in Baylor's victories, Confederate leaders in El Paso were now much more confident that their cause would triumph in New Mexico.[6]

During the summer of 1861 the Mescalero Apaches were quick to capitalize on the war between the whites; under Nicolas's leadership they greatly increased their raids on the mail route in the Fort Davis area. Patrick McCarthy, the sutler and postmaster at Fort Davis, decided that he would try to befriend the Mescaleros and persuaded Nicolas to visit the fort under a flag of truce. He was welcomed as a brother, and there was a great feast, a smoke, and pledges to support a peace treaty. McCarthy and Nicolas then boarded a stage for El Paso, and at Fort Bliss the Apache leader received a royal welcome. Following a formal banquet, Baylor, McCarthy, and Magoffin made speeches about friendship and fraternal love. Nicolas, saying his heart was full of love, signed a peace treaty and then boarded a coach with McCarthy for the return trip. When McCarthy fell asleep, Nicolas jerked his revolvers from their holsters and jumped from the coach. The rest of that summer of 1861 was a prolonged exercise in horror.[7]

On 1 August 1861, by proclamation "To the People of the Territory of Arizona" Baylor assumed the military governorship. He confirmed the people in their rights, continued such laws as were consistent with those of the Confederate States, located the seat of government, and announced appointments to various offices. The Confederate Congress endorsed this action and in January 1862 enacted a law for the organization of the territory of Arizona.[8]

In the meantime, about when Baylor arrived at Fort Bliss, Henry Hopkins Sibley was commissioned a brigadier general in the army of the Confederacy with instructions to raise a brigade to drive Federal forces from New Mexico. Born in Natchitoches, Louisiana, and possessed of a distinguished career, Sibley was holding a command at Taos, New Mexico, when he decided to offer his services to the South. At Hart's Mill in June 1861 he held lengthy discussions with Hart, Magoffin, and Crosby, and concluded that the Federal army was inefficient, that virtually all the American population in the area was pro-Southern, that the native Mexican-Americans would either come to his aid, or at least not hinder his efforts, and that he could depend on the Mesilla and El Paso valleys to furnish supplies. Hart said he had stored forty to fifty thousand pounds of flour across the river. Confident of Sibley's leadership and what he hoped to accomplish, the three El Pasoans at the Hart's Mill conference provided him with the information he wanted to hear.[9]

Sibley established his headquarters in San Antonio in August 1861 and began organizing his staff. Two of Magoffin's sons, Joseph and Samuel, received staff appointments, Joseph as a lieutenant and Samuel as a volunteer aide-de-camp with the rank of major. Sibley also took the first steps for supplying his army once it arrived in Confederate Arizona. Josiah Crosby and Simeon Hart, designated as agents to provide a food supply, authorized purchasing officials to gather feed corn and flour for the army and established Forts Davis, Quitman, and Bliss as storage depots for Sibley's brigade. Sibley sent officers to New Orleans to obtain hard cash to pay Mexican and Arizonan vendors.[10]

Sibley's supply requirements, noted Donald Frazier, seemed achievable. Hart and Crosby assigned purchasing agents to travel to Chihuahua and Sonora to buy corn, flour, salt, beef, soap, and beans. Moreover, Hart had increased production from his own mills, turning out some fifty thousand pounds of flour for the Confederate cause. In his letter to Sibley of 27 October 1861, Hart wrote that he had some forty or fifty thousand dollars at hand, almost all of which he had to send immediately to Sonora to pay for flour and other goods. At the suggestion of Colonel Baylor, he hired an express to travel into Sonora to learn whether Union forces were coming from California by way of Guaymas or Fort Union. Through the express he was ordering the purchase of additional flour, beans, salt, beef, soap, corn, and other goods. He had ten thousand pounds of corn and three hundred thousand pounds of flour for Sibley's brigade. Hart assured Sibley that he could obtain sufficient supplies from Sonora "until such time as you may be in full possession of New Mexico, and can avail yourself of its resources."[11]

On 14 December 1861 General Sibley, having established his temporary headquarters at Fort Bliss, assumed command of all Confederate forces in Texas at Fort Quitman and points north and in the territories of Arizona and New Mexico. Colonel Baylor, however, was to continue exercising the functions of civil and military governor of Arizona. In El Paso Josiah Crosby joined Sibley's staff as acting chief quartermaster, while Magoffin served as a volunteer aide.[12]

In late 1861 Sibley declared his intention to incorporate the north Mexican states into the Confederacy through military occupation, though with the consent of the provincial governors. Colonel James Reily was ordered to proceed to Chihuahua and

Sonora to enlist their aid and support. Governor Luis Terrazas of Chihuahua, after graciously receiving Reily in January 1861 and agreeing to make supplies available to Sibley, stipulated that all sales must be in hard cash. He also said that if orders came from Mexico City, he would be obliged to let Federal troops march through his state. The governor had been caught in the midst of three forces—the Union, the Confederacy, and Mexico.[13]

Colonel Reily then left for the capital of Sonora and the palace of Governor Don Ignacio Pesqueira. He was warmly received and given several concessions to benefit the Confederacy. Unfortunately for Reily, an enterprising reporter for the *San Francisco Bulletin* managed to steal copies of the colonel's letter of introduction from Sibley, as well as some of his notes, and transmit them to General George Wright in California. Within days Wright had a gunboat standing off the harbor at Guaymas and a letter prepared for Pesqueira declaring that "under no circumstances will the Government of the United States permit the rebel hordes to take refuge in Sonora." He went on to state, "I have an army of ten thousand men ready to pass the frontier and protect your government and your people." Pesqueira then sent a letter to Wright promising that if any rebels set foot on Mexican soil, he would exterminate them.[14]

To make matters worse for Sibley, in early 1862, while laying plans for an offensive, he learned to his dismay that Baylor's men had consumed practically all goods in the immediate area and that Hart and Crosby had failed to store sufficient supplies from Mexico. Though foodstuffs and other items were plentiful in Mexico, the Mexicans refused payment in Confederate scrip; Sibley, who had no specie on hand, could make no purchases. Even the natives of New Mexico were reluctant to accept anything but hard cash. Even so, Sibley was confident that his victories in New Mexico would provide for all his needs. Greatly underrating the Union army in New Mexico, Sibley planned to move into the territory, destroy what resistance he might encounter, and seize all Union garrisons, forts, and supply depots, one by one.[15]

The first week in February found Sibley at Fort Thorn with only two and a half regiments of poorly armed, badly clothed, and ill-fed men. By this time some of Sibley's weaknesses as a general and strategist had begun to manifest themselves. He failed dismally to assess realities, and poor health and overindulgence greatly jeopardized his efficiency as a commander. At Valverde, near Socorro, New Mexico, he engaged Union forces under the command of Lieutenant Colonel E. R. S. Canby and won a victory, though at heavy cost. Confederate forces then occupied Albuquerque and Santa Fe, but Canby, with reinforcements just received, retaliated and defeated Sibley's forces at Glorieta Pass, Pigeon's Point, and Apache Canyon, inflicting terrible losses on the Confederates.

"Much of the blame for the failure of the campaign lay on the shoulders of General Sibley," wrote Jerry Thompson. Underestimating his enemy, according to Thompson, was Sibley's gravest error. He also had a poor understanding of Union sentiments in the West, in California and in Colorado mining camps, and of Hispanic New Mexicans, who tended to be either indifferent to the Southern cause or openly pro-Union. Sibley did not understand the politics of northern Mexico, particularly regarding his hope of obtaining supplies from merchants in Sonora and Chihuahua. Finally, he "made a serious mistake in placing blind faith in the ability of his secessionist friends, Josiah F. Crosby and Simeon Hart, to stockpile huge quantities of foodstuffs at Fort Bliss."[16]

May and June 1862 brought the famous march of the California Volunteers, or California Column. Some fourteen hundred troops commanded by Colonel (then Brigadier General) James H. Carleton were ordered to restore Union control over Arizona and New Mexico, and by June one column had reached the Rio Grande. By July the Confederates had abandoned Mesilla, Las Cruces, and Fort Bliss, leaving the latter in a shambles. Some, like Magoffin, left for San Antonio; others crossed the river to El Paso del Norte. Union forces occupied Fort Bliss on 20 August

1862 and raised the United States flag over the post for the first time in a year and a half. The California Column occupied the area until February 1865, when the United States Army took control.[17]

In June 1862 General Carleton placed New Mexico under martial law, and General Canby, commander of Union forces in New Mexico, extended the policy to include El Paso. As a result, military courts in both places assumed authority over all criminal and most civil cases. Congressional legislation provided for the confiscation of the property of any person engaged in armed rebellion or aiding rebellion against the United States.

Proceedings were soon begun that led to the seizure of property belonging to Southern sympathizers, including El Pasoans such as Magoffin, Crosby, and Hart. Most cases were brought against Texans in the federal district court at Mesilla, Doña Ana County, New Mexico Territory. Since the civil courts had ceased to function in El Paso County, the Union occupation forces constituted the sole authority. Thus, with the support of Judge Joab Houghton of the Third Judicial District, Marshal Abraham Cutler immediately declared that his jurisdiction in the Customs District of El Paso del Norte, comprising New Mexico and El Paso County, provided him with the necessary authority.[18]

Shortly before Magoffin left with Confederate forces in early 1862, he moved his wife Dolores to the Mexican side of the river. On 14 July she wrote a letter to her brother, Don Luis Valdez, to report that several Americans and Mexicans had removed all the doors and windows of the Magoffin home and carried them to the other side of the river. She urged her brother to take action and repair as much of the damage as possible to spare her the protests her husband would undoubtedly make on his return from San Antonio. Don Tomás Irigoyen had reported the damage to her and knew who the culprits were.[19]

On 18 July Don Luis wrote Magoffin that as soon as Confederate troops arrived at the ranch of Don Tomás Irigoyen on 3 July they had begun to remove the doors and windows of the Magoffin home. Don Tomás, he reported, had been involved in the destruction, along with his sons and his ranch hands. Don Luis continued:

> Night and day with hatchets and picks they removed all
> of the doors and windows they could. Along with the
> Mexicans were six Americans from Irigoyen's ranch.
> Since most of the doors and windows were taken to the
> Mexican side, I asked Lolita to give me a letter signed in
> your name to permit me to recover as much as possible.
> I have reported all this to the Jefe Político who offered
> to do what he could to help. But of all the thieves who
> took everything from your house, destroying and leav-
> ing everything in a thousand pieces, the greatest
> scoundrel of all is Don Tomás whom you trusted and
> put in charge along with his sons and the rest of the
> thieves.[20]

With Union forces in control of El Paso and Fort Bliss, his home in ruins, his family in El Paso del Norte, and his two sons serving as majors in the Confederate army, Magoffin left the El Paso area to assume the office of state senator in the Confederate government. His son Samuel resigned his commission in 1863, but several months later, when he was on his way to marry Miss Sallie Woolfolk, a Federal patrol sighted him. While attempting to escape he was stricken with apoplexy and died shortly after. His younger brother Joseph served in New Mexico, Virginia, and Texas, and in 1864 married Miss Octavia MacGreal of Houston.[21]

While in the Austin–San Antonio area in 1864–65, Magoffin renewed his correspondence with his good friend and business partner, José Cordero. In view of the losses Magoffin had sustained, Cordero in his letter of 30 March 1864 urged his associate to return to Matamoros and reestablish the lucrative cotton trade between Texas and Mexico that had been so successful in the past. Moreover, Magoffin received a most touching and memorable letter at this time from an old friend and dedicated fellow

Confederate, Augustus B. O'Bannon. Writing from Monterrey on
25 July 1865, shortly after the Civil War came to a close, he said:

My Dear General:

I have received two letters from you since my arrival
here and am glad to learn that you intend returning this
way to Chihuahua and El Paso. It is to be hoped that
President Johnson will relent from his proscriptive
policy by not confiscating property and imprisoning
those who have been fighting for the Independence of
the South. Johnson has sense enough to know that our
cause for secession was not only just and proper, but that
we would have been applauded by the whole world had
we succeeded. It is true I dislike being exiled from my
native country, but I prefer it to proscription and imprisonment. No doubt but that I shall be censored for holding a civil office under President Davis, but I feel proud
in knowing that I discharged my duty faithfully and hon-
estly for the Government I was serving. I held the same
office for many years under the Government of the
United States, but I was faithful and true to the trust
reposed in me. I shall, however, keep in exile until I can
find out that I am not to be punished for serving the late
Confederate States.

I have some means but not much, and hope sincerely
that those of my friends with whom I deposited money
will not defraud me out of it in my old days, but restore
that which I entrusted to their honor and high position
in this changeful world. To betray me now would not
only be robbery but a shameful disregard of all honor
and utter disregard of long cherished friendships.

Monterey is a beautiful city and contains many families of distinction and considerable wealth. There is a
fine theatre here, and is nightly crowded with a fashion-

able and intelligent audience. The actors are from the City of Mexico and evidently understand their business. Indeed I have been as well entertained here as I ever was in the United States.

The French are in peaceful possession of the city and surrounding country, and are governing the same with entire satisfaction to the people.

Should you conclude to return again to our long deserted homes I hope you will not be long before starting, and take this city in your route. I would like to have your company as you are always cheerful, and consequently would dispel much of the gloom which hangs over me.

Colonel Lawrence W. O'Bannon is here, but entirely without means. His wife is in Marshall and no doubt in the same condition. Revolutions are terrible things, humbling the rich as well as those in high places. Consequently they should be a warning to those who are to come after us and fill our places. If these things be true, and that they are so, we have but one adequate support for the calamities of mortal life, and that is a belief that the proception of our fate, however sad or disturbed, is ordered by a Being, whose everlasting purposes embrace all accidents, converting them to good. Let us then adore in humbleness and sincerity of heart and keep the commandants [*sic*] of that Being who has power to make us happy even amid the many vicissitudes of life; and when we are called to pass through that dark valley which leads to eternity, we shall be guided by His omnipotent hand, and be welcomed by Him and His angels into that Kingdom prepared for the redeemed from the foundation of the world.

Remember me sincerely to Major Dwyer and my friend, his wife, also to Joseph your Son and to Mrs. Dwyer and believe me.[22]

About the time that the Civil War in the United States was coming to a close, the French forces of Napoleon III that controlled most of Mexico forced Benito Juárez, leader of the Liberal cause, to seek refuge with his cabinet in El Paso del Norte where they remained for the rest of the year. Juárez stated that he was establishing the national government of Mexico there so he could take full advantage of Secretary William H. Seward's reversal of policy: strict neutrality was now to be abandoned and the sale of American arms and munitions to the Juárez government allowed. In time the tide began to turn in Juárez's favor. Magoffin, who had remained in the Austin–San Antonio area most of the time, returned to El Paso in mid-1866.[23]

On 2 September 1865 the *Santa Fe Gazette* published the proclamation of Abraham Cutler, marshal of the United States for the territory of New Mexico, against the property of James W. Magoffin for his alleged violation of the legislation of 13 July 1861. The Thirty-Seventh Congress, meeting in extra session beginning on 4 July 1861, had taken steps to bring the might of the nation to suppress the rebellion. Property that was used by or intended to be used to support the Confederacy was to be seized and confiscated. Under this ruling Magoffin, whose property was to be forfeited to the United States, condemned, and sold, was ordered to appear in the federal district court in Mesilla, New Mexico, on 6 November 1865 to present his claims and allegations. The proclamation further ordered the seizure of 1,960 acres extending from San Elizario westward—40 acres in San Elizario, four tracts of 320 acres each known as Magoffinsville, and 640 acres east of the town of Franklin to the juncture of Old River and the Rio Grande.[24]

Magoffin remained in Austin in the latter part of 1865 and became acquainted with Governor A. J. Hamilton, a moderate Republican. Mistakenly assuming that Magoffin had been granted amnesty, on 13 November 1865 the governor issued him a commission empowering him on his return to El Paso to organize a militia company for the maintenance of order and protection of the citizens in the area. So impressed with Magoffin was the governor that he even granted him authority to issue blank commissions to be filled in with the names of people suitable to act as county officials. On 6 December 1865 Magoffin replied to the governor that he had a party of fifteen good men to assist him, but suggested the governor appoint twenty-five to fifty men with a good officer to take command of Fort Bliss. "It would really be to the advantage of the state of the Union," said Magoffin, "if he and the governor could work together civilly and militarily and be united as we should be." On 6 May 1866 Magoffin returned to Fort Bliss armed with Hamilton's carte blanche to reorganize county government.[25]

When Captain David H. Brotherton, commandant at Fort Bliss, refused to allow Magoffin to act on behalf of the state of Texas, Magoffin decided to take his case to Washington in the hope that President Andrew Johnson would grant him executive clemency. On 7 September 1867 President Johnson granted James W. Magoffin a full pardon and amnesty, but included a provision that "he shall not, by virtue of this warrant, claim any property or the proceeds of any property that has been sold by the order, judgment, or decree of a court under the confiscation laws of the United States."[26]

In May 1867 floodwater washed away more than half the newly constructed quarters and all the corrals and storehouses at Fort Bliss. This forced the army to abandon the Magoffinsville site and move into quarters on Concordia Ranch, about a mile below the former site and on a bluff sixteen feet above the level of the river. Nearby was the residence of Hugh Stephenson, former owner of the ranch, and now the home of two of Stephenson's married daughters, Adelaide Zabriskie and Benancia French. At length Adelaide's husband, James, negotiated a lease for twenty-five hundred dollars a year.[27]

"The Fort Bliss of 1869," wrote Lydia Spenser Lane, who had been so charmed with the former post at Magoffinsville in 1857, "was not the one we knew and enjoyed so much. Great inroads had been made by the Rio Grande: some of the buildings were washed away. . . . Our old house still stood, but the roof had fallen in. The others were masses of crumbling adobe. What changes had taken place since we were all so happy there a few years before!"[28]

Since 1862 Magoffin had lost a son, his home, Fort Bliss, and property amounting to 1,960 acres. Although President Johnson granted him amnesty in 1867, Captain Brotherton again denied Magoffin the political authority in El Paso that the governor of Texas had given him. Suffering greatly from dropsy, he sensed the end was near. On 1 September 1868 he conveyed to Joseph all his property, which had been confiscated three years before. He died in San Antonio on 27 September 1868. Following services at the San Fernando Cathedral, he was buried in the family vault on the ranch of Joseph Dwyer, his son-in-law.[29]

CONCLUSION

The year 1999 marks the two-hundredth anniversary of the birth of James Wiley Magoffin, El Paso's greatest pioneer. For more than a century, by reason of his dedication and contribution to the development of the El Paso area and his principal accomplishments to ensure its future, Magoffin's place in the history of the area has remained unchallenged.

A brief summary of these accomplishments must include the following: 1. For twenty-five years, Magoffin was one of the great names engaged in mercantile activities on the Chihuahua Trail. 2. He played a decisive role in the war with Mexico that made possible the conquest of New Mexico by American forces, facilitating the occupation of Santa Fe without a fight. 3. He founded Magoffinsville, the American El Paso and nucleus for the future town of El Paso, Texas. 4. He assisted in the establishment of Fort Bliss, thus initiating El Paso's well-known military tradition. 5. He supported the Confederate cause, primarily because of its commitment to a southern transcontinental railroad that would ensure El Paso's future. 6. He left a legacy to his son Joseph for the development of El Paso—the Continental Crossroads—with its distinctive bilingual, bicultural traditions.

In spite of Magoffin's commanding role in the history of El Paso and the American Southwest, however, historians have generally neglected him. The full-length biographical treatment that he so obviously deserved never appeared; Rex Strickland's *Six Who Came to El Paso* has remained the sole detailed reference on the area's most important founding father for the past thirty years.

In the meantime, however, helping to keep the Magoffin name alive and visible has been the Magoffin Home, the large adobe structure that Magoffin's son Joseph built in the mid-1870s and that family members have continuously owned and used for more than a century. In 1976 the City of El Paso and the Texas

Parks and Wildlife Department purchased the home and its 1.5 acres of grounds to develop it as a historic site and to preserve its significance as the residence of one of the most important and influential families of west Texas in the late nineteenth and twentieth centuries. In 1994 the Texas Parks and Wildlife Department published *Magoffin Home State Historic Site* that includes information on the home, the Magoffin family, and the rich collection of historical materials at the site.[1]

My research on Magoffin the past several years has revealed these important findings: 1. State Department records in the Center for Southwest Studies at the University of New Mexico Library reveal that Magoffin never served as American consul at Saltillo because the appointment made by the Department of State was never received. 2. For fourteen years, 1821 to 1835, Magoffin was a young merchant heavily involved in the lucrative Texas trade, according to the Despatches from United States Consuls in Matamoros. 3. The Béxar Archives have documents covering Magoffin's relations with Mexican officials in 1835, and disclose details on the merchandise Magoffin shipped to Chihuahua prior to his departure from Texas that year. 4. Documents concerning the Magoffin-Curcier relationship, whose business supplied the Santa Rita de Cobre mine from 1835 to 1837, are in the Janos Archive. 5. Magoffin's service as a member of the Ayuntamiento of Chihuahua may be found in the records of that body at the UTEP Library. 6. The Juárez Archive provides a Mexican point of view for matters such as the names of Americans engaged in merchant and/or mining activities in Mexico, details involving Magoffin's capture in 1846, Mexican defensive measures to check Doniphan, and a Mexican account of the Battle of Brazito. 7. Finally, the Glasgow Collection in the Magoffin Home has a thirteen-page financial record of the Chihuahua trade partnership of James Magoffin and José Cordero, 1849 to 1858, that imported European merchandise through the firm of Peter Harmony Nephews and Company. Also found in this important collection are letters to Magoffin from Francisco Elguea, member of the prominent copper mining family of Chihuahua; from Magoffin's brother Samuel; from his brother-in-law Isaac Lightner; and from his dear friend, Augustus B. O'Bannon.

DOCUMENTARY APPENDIX

Appointment of James W. Magoffin as United States Consul at Saltillo, Mexico.*

His Excellency

The President of the United States

We, the undersigned, take the liberty of recommending to your Excellency Mr. James W. McGoffin of Kentucky as a suitable person to fill the vacancy of the U.S. consulate in Acapulco, in Mexico, occasioned by the decease of the late incumbent. In presenting this gentleman for your patronage, we do it with full assurance, that his merit and qualifications render him worthy of it, and that the interests of the Government, as far as connected with this office, would be promoted by committing it to his charge. Allied to some of the best and most distinguished families of our State, and possessing great excellence of personal character, he commands, as he deserves, respect and esteem. His commercial education and pursuits peculiarly fit him for the duties of a consulate, which we doubt not he would perform advantageously to the General Government. Believing as we do that this gentleman would be found to have merited your patronage, we indulge the hope that you may find it convenient to grant him the office for which we here submit our application.

With sentiments of the
highest consideration
we have the honor to be your
Excellency's Very Obt Servts

Washington
December 13, 1824

T P Moon
Robt R Henry
Sam Houston
F F Barbour

Robt Latimer
J F Johnson
R A Buckner
Isham Talbot
R M Johnson

James W. McGoffin Esq. Consul of the U.S. for the port of Saltillo
Department of State
Washington 3 March 1825
Sir,

The President by and with the advice and consent of the Senate, having appointed you Consul of the United States for the port of Saltillo in Mexico, I have the honor of enclosing herewith your Commission, accompanied with printed Consular instructions and a blank Consular Bond, which you will execute on your part and forward to the United States to be filled up, taking care to have a certificate from the District Attorney on the state in which the sureties reside subjoined to the Bond that they are in his opinion sufficient before it is transmitted to this office.

I am very respectfully, Sir,
Your obedt Servt
(Signed) John Quincy Adams

(Department of State Circular dated 15 January 1830 was forwarded to James W. McGoffin, Consul of the U.S. at Saltillo, Mexico, on that same day.)

(Department of State Circular dated 26 May 1830 was forwarded to James W. McGoffin, Consul, U.S. Saltillo, Mexico.)

(Department of State Circular dated 24 May 1831 was forwarded to James W. McGoffin, Consul, Saltillo.)

(Department of State Circular dated 1 January 1834 was forwarded to J. W. McGoffin at Saltillo.)

James W. McGoffin, esq.   Department of State
U. S. Consul, Saltillo, Mexico   Washington, 7 April 1834

Sir,

The object of this letter is to inquire the cause of your silence, and to ascertain whether the Instructions to Consuls, and other forms which were forwarded to all our Consuls ever reached you.

Circulars of the 1st of February and 16th of January were sent to your consulate.

I am, sir, respectfully your obedt servant
Louis McLane

*Center for Southwest Studies, University of New Mexico Library.

Information concerning Magoffin's appointment as Consul at Saltillo received by the Chihuahua Government, 10 May 1831.*

(Translation)
Circular of the Supreme Government of the State, 24 April 1831. It has received information that Santiago Magoffin of the United States of North America has been named Consul for the City of Saltillo. National Legislature, Real de San Lorenzo, 10 May 1831.

Demetrio Ontiveros,
Secretary

*Juárez Archive (microfilm, UTEP Library, MF513R23F160).

Letter from James Magoffin to his brother Manuel (Samuel) reporting on his activities in Chihuahua, 3 December 1832.*

Saml Magoffin

    Dear Sir

    I send you a few lines by McMaster and hope they will find you well. I have been back from Morelos 6 weeks and have made an arrangement with Harrison which is this. He takes all my goods on hand and a bar of Silver which I have & my balance he has promised to wait with me 2 years, which will be I presume between 2 & 3000 I intend taking up my old note I gave him a new one due 2 years after date. I think by that time I will be able to pay him up. I received a letter from you dated 3 m° back informing me of your having sent me a small box of Liquors which arrived here 3 weeks since. Duke was detained by bad roads & high watters—the Brandy Drinks with the Sardines. Oh Lord dont talk Chihuahua is a hell of a place as all the boys gamble like the Devil. We have an English preacher here who puts his $5 & 6 down on the King for the Duce. Oh we have a fine lot of Boys. You Matamoros gentlemen have no Idea of Our Commerce as it consists mostly in Cards & Of all the foreigners their is not one but what goes to his Death On Monty every Day I believe Mr. Curcier has a notion of starting a Monty if he does I leave town Our Friend Willis is in Alamo & doing tolerable well has one thin 2 thousand doll^s I am going their in about 12 Days from this time to join him in a tour through the warm country & will not be back to this place until March as we expect to got to Masaclan no person knows what my intention is I tell them I am going to Jesus Maria, as that is on the road to Alamos I think if we have any thing like good fortune we can make $10,000 in the trip we understand each other well & I know he is not a *flat*. If I succeed as well as I think I will I can buy goods to my notion in the port of Masaclan shall lay our money out their—I am not afraid of making a loosing trip at any rate & if we get good betting at the games I must win as we can play it when both together very strong—My prospects now I think are tollerable fair for making a raise & if I can get hold of 10 or 15 thousand I know I can keep it Payne and Douglass made 30,000 in that part of the world & they cannot have the advantages that we will have I send you a file your friend Don Juan A Pareja wants you to have him brought from N.O. 330 of the fances kind also 144 Files of different kinds *para abrir letres* the last you will have to see some person that understands the kind they are—for the Mint he pays me 25 per *M* upon all charges delivered in this place Pareja is now the manager of the Mint & you must try & send them to him as Soon as possible also the Watch Seal Such a one as you had for Don Vincent Palacios who will pay the Cost here he is Secretary of State & I would be glad you would send him one If you have an opportunity a first rate Fayton of the 1st Watter with 2 setts of Harness such a one as will Cost in N. O. $350 these are articles that I can make 100 pr ct on If I think proper to Sell them they are much better than Martes & Hanan If you are not too hard run I would be glad to have the fayton but for godsake dont forget the Barrels & boxes. Your Brother

J. W. Magoffin

(In the margin)

The Ladies send their compliments to you also Josefita & Manuelito a Boy who is 4 m° old he is a hell of a fellow I shall write you by mail write me often as my letters will be sent in from here I cant imagine why you are so neglectful in writing.

*Glasgow Collection, Magoffin Home.

A report of Anglo-American violations of Mexican laws, 19 July 1835, by the First Section of Field Operations.*

(Translation)

Citizen don Luciano García, who has just returned to this town of El Paso del Norte has notified me that some Anglo-Americans have brought into this territory a considerable number of mules for trading purposes on the Mimbres River. In the Cristobal territory they caused a stampede led by Don Miguel Maike, and their behavior is outrageous and damaging, contrary to the orders and decrees of his Excellency, the Sr. Governor and Commandant General of this state, for whom I enclose a printed notice that requires your seal so that these foreigners will not brazenly ridicule the provisions which have been prescribed. You may wish to order an inspection of the above mentioned animals and their brands to verify if they have been stolen from the state. The Americans have captured unmarked mules and branded them as their owners. One of these Americans is named Don Santiago. He has a copper trade, and leaves his mules in the Sierra Fuerte to be branded. He supplies the Apaches with gunpowder, and all of this information I plan to give to the commandant. You will recognize the bitter situation the state is in and the protection the foreigners enjoy in their alliance with the savage Indians. They pacify the Comanches with arms and munitions, and it is to be regretted that Mexicans are making fun of our laws and decrees. I am giving an account of all this to his Excellency, the Governor and Commandant General.

July 19, 1835. José María Ronquillo, Political Chief and Military Commandant of the Territory of New Mexico. Copied in Chihuahua August 13, 1835. Antonio Rey, Secretary.

*Juárez Archive (microfilm, UTEP Library, MF495R5).

Inventory of James Magoffin's personal effects after his arrest in El Paso del Norte, 23 November 1846.*

(Translation)

1 rifle of 2 keys with lock and powder flask
1 brace of pistols
1 plain knife
1 wagon, battered with straps broken
1 trunk, broken and battered
1 sun shade (tarpaulin)
1 iron skillet
1 tin plated coffee pot
1 knife sharpener
1 pair of mules
1 hide
2 bottles
4 tin plated boxes
3 canisters
1 cart canister
1 basket with six bottles
1 piece of cheese

1 bushel basket with a little coffee
1 large box of wood
1 suitcase
1 gunny sack
4 brushes
1 small amount of tea
1 canister of spices
2 letter cases
1 inkwell
8 pens
1 small bit of rice
1 bottle of medicine
1 jug of cathartic salt
2 gloves
1 bit of wool
1 piece of ham
1 hair brush

Total Value: 479.43 pesos
El Paso del Norte

November 23, 1846
(Signed) Sebastián Bermúdez

*Juárez Archive (microfilm, UTEP Library, MF495F172).

Petition of J. W. Magoffin to Col. Joseph K. F. Mansfield, inspector of western military posts, on behalf of the property owners and merchants opposing the removal of troops, 20 November 1849.*

We the undersigned owners of property and merchants residing in the vicinity of El Paso, or the U.S. Post Opposite to El Paso, beg respectfully to submit to Your Excellency.

That we have recently heard that an order has been issued to vacate the land at present occupied by U.S. Troops opposite to El Paso, which would leave this part of the country totally unprotected; that such a measure is not only highly detrimental to our interests, but injuring the interests of the whole neighboring county, and your petitioners respectfully beg that you will reconsider said order, and give your attention to the following as a few of the reasons why the present post should be continued.

The removal of the troops to San Elizario, 25 miles below this point (and where there is already a small force quite sufficient in our opinion for the protection of that town) would leave exposed to the depredations of the Indians a large amount of property of American citizens, at present accumulated here, there being besides animals and other descriptions of property at least the value of three hundred thousand dollars of merchandise in this immediate vicinity.

From its geographical position in the mountain pass this post would continue to be the real thoroughfare for emigrants to California as well as the principal depot for traders with Mexico and the county above and below this, whilst the post of San Elizario is situated about 20 miles off from the main road.

The vacating of this post will we think cause all the new settlements between Donna Anna and Isleta to be abandoned for the want of protection not only from the Indians, but from a large band of outlaws of all nations now infesting the town of El Paso, who openly bid defiance to the authorities of that place and will undoubtedly extend their operations to this side of the river, should we be left without protection.

The agricultural interests of this neighborhood are now rapidly advancing to a prosperous condition, and a number of farms which would add largely to the products of the county are to be opened in the valleys above and below this point during the coming season, but these will necessarily be abandoned should our protection be withdrawn.

The present post is situated on the banks of the Rio Grande immediately at the principal ford, and every opportunity is here obtained to maintain order among the lawless of our own nation who often accompany emigrants to California, but cannot from this place escape the authority whilst from San Elizario they can easily evade pursuit. Moreover, we deem it incumbent upon our Government to give incidental protection at least, to the Mexican Territory, which is effectively done at this post, but would in no manner be accomplished if San Elizario were the only post for our troops.

The advantages of this post for obtaining supplies and the comfortable accommodation of the troops will of course have been represented to Your Excellency from other sources, but the undersigned are satisfied that the U.S. Troops cannot now have in this County more pleasant and comfortable quarters than they are at present occupying, being in that respect far superior to those that could be had at San Elizario. All of which is respectfully submitted to your consideration.

> We are, Colonel,
> Very respectfully
> J. W. Magoffin
> (Ten additional names)

*New Mexico State Records Center and Archives.

Report of J. W. Magoffin to the Committee of El Paso County, Texas, concerning Indian depredations.*

Gentlemen,

Believing it is the duty of every citizen to give all true information respecting Indian hostilities on our frontier as requested for the present year, I proceed, and I shall confine myself particularly to my own losses, without mentioning many others, too numerous to mention, sustained by those who were much less able to bear them than myself amongst whom are many good citizens reduced to a state of poverty by the savage. Since Jan 1st this year I have lost 60 mules taken within 150 yds of my house, the 1st lot was taken in the direction of the Coppermines, the 2nd to the Sacramento mountain. About the 1st March they took from my Ranche (Canutilla) 15 miles from El Paso and 30 miles from Fort Fillmore, on the main road to Santa Fe all my stock of cattle, killing one man and taking off a boy, say 16 years old. On the 25th of July they made a 2nd attack on my Ranche about 10 a m taking all the outfit I had there for farming purposes, Cows, Calves, et., etc. Indians about 60 in number.

I have since that time received no further damage from them but daily hear of their terrible outrages committed upon citizens on both sides of the River

Respectfully yours

Magoffinsville Texas   (Signed) JW Magoffin
August 5, 1852

*Governors' Papers: Peter H. Bell, Texas State Archives.

U.S. Marshal's proclamation confiscating the property of James W. Magoffin, 2 September 1865.*

United States of America
3rd Judicial District of
The Territory of N.M.

I, Abraham Cutler, Marshall of the United States for the Territory of New Mexico, do hereby give public notice that, in the case

THE UNITED STATES, libellant

Against

The property of James W. Magoffin, to wit:

The following described property situated in the El Paso County State of Texas

viz:

A certain tract of land situated in the Town of San Elizario bounded on the south and east by the lands of Doña Viviana Bareta; on the north by the lands of Tomas Sanchez and on the west by the main San Antonio street or road which separates it from the lands of Juan Ruiz containing 40 acres more or less.

Also a certain tract of land about 1 1/2 miles east of the Town of Franklin, described as follows:

Beginning at a stake on the bank of the Rio Grande, set for the lower corner of survey No. 1 as made by Robert H. Hays from which a cottonwood 10 inches in diameter bears N. 45 degrees E. 11 varas; thence north 1430 1/2 varas to a stake and mound; thence east 672 varas to a stake and mound, thence south 2945 1/2 varas to a stake from which a cottonwood six inches in diameter bears N. 10 1/2 degrees E. 15 varas; thence up the Rio Grande with its meanders to the place of beginning or however else the same may be bounded and described and containing 320 acres more or less.

Also a certain tract of land near the last above described, described and bounded as follows

viz:

Beginning at a stake on the bank of the Rio Grande set for the lower corner of survey No. 53 from which a cottonwood 6 inches in diameter bears N. 10 1/2 degrees E. 15 varas; thence north 2563 varas to a stake on the bank of the Rio Grande from which a Mesquite on a hillock bears N. 45 degrees E. 8 varas; thence up the Rio Grande with its meanders to the place of beginning or however else the same may be bounded or described and containing 320 acres more or less.

Also a certain tract of land adjoining the last above described and described as follows, viz:

Beginning at a stake on the bank of the Rio Grande for the upper or southwest corner of survey No. 57 from which a Tornillo or Screw tree 4 inches in diameter bears N. 20 degrees E. 10 varas, another Tornillo bears S. 15 degrees E. 15 varas; thence north 2442 1/2 varas to a stake and mound; thence west 534 varas to a stake and mound; thence south 2926 1/2 varas to a stake on the bank of the Rio Grande from which a Tornillo or Screw tree bears N. 2 degrees W. 25 varas, another Tornillo or Screw tree bears N. 15 1/2 degrees W. 13 varas; thence down the Rio Grande with its meanders to the place of beginning or however else the same may be bounded or described and containing 320 acres more or less, together with all the buildings, houses and corrals attached, and all of the rents and immunities due or belonging to any of the above described property. Upon the four last above described tracts of land is situated Magoffinsville and they are known as the Magoffinsville property.

Also a certain tract of land as surveys numbered 11 and 12 containing 640 acres of land more or less, and situated about 4 miles east from the Town of Franklin upon the Rio Grande near the Junction of Old River and the Rio Grande, or however else the same may be bounded or described.

The same being libelled in the United States District Court for the 3rd Judicial District of the Territory of New Mexico in a case of seizure and forfeiture for alleged violation of the acts of Congress approved July 13, 1861, and at other times since that time; and I hereby give further notice that the time assigned for the return of said warrant and the hearing of this cause is the first Monday, the sixth day of November A.D. 1865, and I hereby admonish and summon all persons claiming any interest in said property or knowing or have anything to say why the same should not be decreed to be forfeited to the United States and be condemned and sold to answer the prayer of said Libel that they be and appear before said District Court at the Court House in La Mesilla in said district on the 6th day of November A.D. 1865 at 10 o'clock A.M. when and where said cause will be heard there and then to interpose their claim and answer said Libel and make their allegation in that behalf.

La Mesilla, New Mexico
September 2, 1865

ABRAHAM CUTLER
U.S. Marshal

Santa Fe Gazette, 2 September 1865.

Pardon of James W. Magoffin by President Andrew Johnson.*

To all to whom these presents shall come, Greeting:

Whereas, James W. Magoffin of El Paso County, Texas, by taking part in the late rebellion against the Government of the United States, has made himself liable to heavy pains and penalties,

And whereas, the circumstances of his case tender him a proper object of Executive clemency.

Now, therefore, That I, ANDREW JOHNSON, President of the United States of America, in consideration of premises, divers other good and sufficient reasons, me thereunto moving, do grant to the said James W. Magoffin a full pardon and amnesty for all offences by him committed, arising from participation, direct or implied, in the said rebellion, conditioned as follows:

1st. This pardon to be of no effect until the said James W. Magoffin shall take the oath prescribed in the Proclamation of the President, dated May 29, 1865.

2nd. To be void and of no effect if the said James W. Magoffin shall hereafter, at any time, acquire any property whatever in slaves, or make use of slave labor.

3rd. That the said James W. Magoffin first pay all costs which may have accrued in any proceedings instituted or pending against his person or property before the date of the acceptance of this warrant.

4th. That the said James W. Magoffin shall not, by virtue of this warrant, claim any property or the proceeds of any property that has been sold by the order, judgment, or decree of a court under the confiscation laws of the United States.

5th. That the said James W. Magoffin shall notify the Secretary of State, in writing, that he has received and accepted the foregoing pardon.

In testimony whereof, I have hereunto signed my name and caused the Seal of the United States to be affixed.

Done at the City of Washington, this Seventh day of September, A.D. 1867,

and of the Independence of the United States
the Ninety-second.
Andrew Johnson
By the President: William H. Seward
Secretary of State

Washington City
September 10, 1867

Honorable William H. Seward
    Secretary of State
                            Sir:
                                    I have the honor to
acknowledge the receipt of the President's Warrant of Pardon,
bearing date September Seventh, 1867, and hereby signify my
acceptance of the same, with all the conditions therein specified.

I am, Sir,

Your obedient servant,
J. W. Magoffin

***Center for Southwest Studies, University of New Mexico
Library.**

NOTES

INTRODUCTION

1. John L. Waller, "James Wiley Magoffin," in *The Handbook of Texas*, edited by Walter Prescott Webb (Austin, 1962), 2:130–31.

2. Rex Strickland, *Six Who Came to El Paso: Pioneers of the 1840s* (El Paso, 1963), 29–34.

3. J. J. Bowden, "The Magoffin Salt War," *Password* 43 (summer 1962): 95–121.

CHAPTER ONE

1. Robert L. Kincaid, *The Wilderness Road* (Indianapolis, 1947), 11–13.

2. Thomas D. Clark, *A History of Kentucky* (Lexington, Ky., 1960), 36–59.

3. Ibid., 85.

4. E. W. Gould, *Fifty Years on the Mississippi* (St. Louis, 1889), 194; Thomas D. Clark, *The Kentucky* (New York, 1942), 61-68.

5. "Joseph Magoffin" in the Biographical and Historical Sketchbook of the Pioneers' Association of El Paso County, Texas (University of Texas at El Paso [UTEP] Library, 1932), 56; Magoffin Family File, Pioneers' Sketch Book Harrodsburg Historical Society, Harrodsburg, Kentucky.

6. The Territorial Papers of the United States (Washington, D.C., 1938): The Territory of Mississippi, 6:573, 579, 627, 722, 724; The Territory of Alabama, 18:198, 357, 521, 523, 668; The Territory of Arkansas, 19:134. Eugene C. Barker, *The Life of Stephen F. Austin* (Dallas, 1925). In the 1820s the Magoffin name was frequently spelled McGoffin; Barker spelled it McGuffin, possibly a transcription error.

7. Grace King, *New Orleans: The Place and the People* (New York, 1968), 259.

8. George Wythe Baylor, "Tales of Don Santiago," *El Paso Herald*, 20 January 1900. Leola Freeman first used Baylor's stories as source material in her typewritten manuscript, "James Wiley Magoffin," written in 1951. Baylor's tales have recently been edited by Jerry D. Thompson in *Into the Far, Wild Country* (El Paso, 1996), 136–39.

9. Baylor, *Into the Far, Wild Country*, 137.

10. David J. Weber, *The Mexican Frontier, 1821–1846* (Albuquerque, 1982), 163–64.

11. Ibid, 24–27.

12. Sam Houston et al. to the President of the United States, Washington, D.C., 13 December 1824, Center for Southwest Studies, University of New Mexico Library, Albuquerque. See Documentary Appendix.

13. Louis McLane to J. W. McGoffin, Washington, D.C., 1 January 1834; Louis McLane to James W. McGoffin, Washington, D.C., 7 April 1834, Center for Southwest Studies.

14. Daniel W. Smith to John Forsyth, Matamoros, 26 May 1834, Despatches from United States Consuls in Matamoros (microfilm, UTEP Library, M281R1F39). Curiously, the El Paso del Norte area had learned of the Saltillo consular position as early as May 1831, as it was published in the state government circular at the Real de San Lorenzo, a short distance east of El Paso del Norte. Circular of the State Government, Real de San Lorenzo, 10 May 1831, Juárez Archive (microfilm, UTEP Library, MF513R23F160).

15. Weber, *The Mexican Frontier*, 166. Noah Smithwick, *The Evolution of a State* (Austin, 1935), 9.

16. Carlos E. Castañeda, *Our Catholic Heritage in Texas, 1519–1936* (Austin, 1936–58), 6:238–42; Weber, *The Mexican Frontier*, 140–41.

17. Daniel W. Smith to Louis McLane, Matamoros, 30 July 1830, Despatches from United States Consuls in Matamoros (microfilm, UTEP Library, M281R1F11).

Chapter Two

1. Daniel W. Smith to Louis McLane, Matamoros, 1 July 1829, Despatches from United States Consuls in Matamoros (microfilm, UTEP Library, M281R1F10).

2. Tom Lea, *The King Ranch* (Boston, 1957), 1:23.

3. Ibid., 1:49.

4. Weber, *The Mexican Frontier*, 166.

5. Ibid.

6. Ohland Morton, *Terán and Texas* (Austin, 1948), 72.

7. Eugene C. Barker, *Mexico and Texas, 1821–1835* (Dallas, 1928), 76–78.

8. Alleine Howren, "Causes and Origin of the Decree of April 6, 1830," *The Southwestern Historical Quarterly* 16 (April 1913): 412.

9. Ibid., 415–16.

10. Frank Wagner, "John Stryker," *The New Handbook of Texas* (Austin, 1996), 6:132.

11. J. W. Magoffin to Samuel Magoffin, Chihuahua, 3 December 1832. Mrs. W. J. Glasgow Collection in the Magoffin Home, El Paso, Texas. Stella Drumm noted that monte was played with cards, the suits being clubs, swords, suns, and cups, all with their own colors and figures. Each suit included ten cards numbered from ace to seven and a knave and horse instead of a queen and king. "The mysteries of the game could be learned only by losing at it," according to Drumm. Stella M. Drumm, ed., *Down the Santa Fe Trail and into Mexico—Diary of Susan Shelby Magoffin, 1846–1847* (Santa Fe, 1975), 120.

12. J. W. Magoffin to Samuel Magoffin, Chihuahua, 3 December 1832, Glasgow Collection. Mention of Curcier's name in the letter is interesting. Magoffin and Curcier formed a partnership in Chihuahua in 1835 involving the shipping of merchandise to the Santa Rita copper mine. See Documentary Appendix.

13. Ibid.

14. Weber, *The Mexican Frontier*, 177–78.

15. Juan N. Almonte, "Statistical Report on Texas," trans. C. E. Castañeda, *Southwestern Historical Quarterly* 28 (January 1925): 193.

16. Daniel W. Smith to Louis McLane, Matamoros, 1 January 1834, Despatches from United States Consuls in Matamoros (microfilm, UTEP Library, M281R1F39).

17. Strickland, *Six Who Came to El Paso*, 27; Drumm, *Down the Santa Fe Trail*, xx.

18. Weber, *The Mexican Frontier*, 248.

19. Four guías of Santiago Magoffin, Velasco, 27 March 1835, Béxar Archives, reel 164, frame 545.

20. The extensive correspondence of Mexican officials involving Magoffin's nonpayment of customs duties is in the Béxar Archives, reel 164, frames 932 and 933; and reel 165, frames 8, 9, 42, 43, 45, 53, 56, 78, 296, 358, and 361. See also John H. Jenkins, ed., *The Papers of the Texas Revolution, 1835–36* (Austin, 1973), 1:101–102.

CHAPTER THREE

1. Max L. Moorhead, *New Mexico's Royal Road* (Norman, Okla., 1958), 63–64, 75; Larry Mahon Beachum, *William Becknell: Father of the Santa Fe Trade* (El Paso, 1982), 29; R. L. Duffus, *The Santa Fe Trail* (New York, 1943), 68; Marc Simmons, *On the Santa Fe Trail* (Lawrence, Kans., 1986), 1.

2. Edward J. Glasgow to Wm. E. Connelley, 2 November 1906, in Mark L. Gardner, ed., *Brothers on the Santa Fe and Chihuahua Trails* (Niwot, Colo., 1993), 186.

3. Moorhead, *New Mexico's Royal Road*, 186–88; interview with Edward J. Glasgow, 11 March 1906, in Gardner, *Brothers on the Santa Fe and Chihuahua Trails*, 207–208.

4. W. H. Timmons, "The El Paso Area in the Mexican Period, 1821–1848," *Southwestern Historical Quarterly* 84 (July 1980): 7.

5. J. W. Magoffin to Wm. B. Jones, Chihuahua, 16 October 1838, National Archives, RG 84.3, Consulate General, Mexican Correspondence.

6. José María Ronquillo to the Jefe Político and Comandante Militar of the Territorio del Nuevo México, 19 July 1835, Juárez Archive (microfilm, UTEP Library, MF495R5).

7. J. J. Bowden, *Spanish and Mexican Land Grants in the Chihuahuan*

Acquisition (El Paso, 1971), 58; Graziella Altamirano and Guadalupe Villa, *Chihuahua: Textos de su historia, 1824–1921* (Mexico City, 1988), 1:339.

8. R. B. Brown, "John Potts of Chihuahua," *Password* 43 (spring 1998): 9–10; A. Wislizenus, *Memoir of a Tour to Northern Mexico Connected with Colonel Doniphan's Expedition in 1846 and 1847* (Albuquerque, 1969), 58.

9. Bowden, *Spanish and Mexican Land Grants*, 58.

10. J. W. Magoffin to Wm. B. Jones, Chihuahua, 30 January and 9 March 1839, National Archives, RG 84.3, Consulate General, Mexican Correspondence.

11. Noel M. Loomis, *The Texan–Santa Fe Pioneers* (Norman, Okla., 1958), 42.

12. William B. Griffen, *Utmost Good Faith: Patterns of Apache-Mexican Hostilities in Northern Chihuahua Border Warfare, 1821–1848* (Albuquerque, 1988), 56–58.

13. Rick Hendricks and W. H. Timmons, *San Elizario: Spanish Presidio to Texas County Seat* (El Paso, 1998), 54–55.

14. W. H. Timmons, *El Paso: A Borderlands History* (El Paso, 1990), 83–84.

15. Hendricks and Timmons, *San Elizario*, 57.

16. Timmons, "The El Paso Area in the Mexican Period," 14–15.

17. Strickland, *Six Who Came to El Paso*, 28.

18. Perry McCandless, *A History of Missouri* (Columbia, Mo., 1972), 2:132.

19. Gardner, *Brothers on the Santa Fe and Chihuahua Trails*, 137–38 n. 1.

20. George Rutledge Gibson, *Journal of a Soldier Under Kearny and Doniphan, 1846–1847*, ed. Ralph P. Bieber (Glendale, Calif., 1935), 98.

21. Moorhead, *New Mexico's Royal Road*, 156–57.

22. William Y. Chalfant, *Dangerous Passage: The Santa Fe Trail and the Mexican War* (Norman, Okla., 1994), 32.

23. Dale Morgan, ed., *Overland in 1846* (Georgetown, Calif., 1963), 2:534.

24. Thomas Hart Benton, *Thirty Years' View* (New York, 1856), 2:683.

25. W. L. Marcy to Colonel S. W. Kearny, 18 June 1846, in Ralph Emerson Twitchell, *The Conquest of Santa Fe*, ed. Bill Tate (Truchas, N. Mex., 1967), 48.

CHAPTER FOUR

1. Moorhead, *New Mexico's Royal Road*, 158–59.

2. Philip St. George Cooke, *The Conquest of New Mexico and California in 1846–1848* (Albuquerque, 1964), 14–15.

3. Ibid., 15, 21, 25–26.

4. Moorhead, *New Mexico's Royal Road*, 159–60.

5. Howard Roberts Lamar, *The Far Southwest, 1846–1912: A Territorial History* (New Haven, 1966), 62.

6. Twitchell, *The Conquest of Santa Fe*, 50.

7. Ibid., 52–54; Mark L. Gardner and Marc Simmons, eds., *The Mexican War Correspondence of Richard Smith Elliot* (Norman, Okla., 1997), 47. Magoffin's letter is printed in its entirety here on pages 41–42.

8. Mark L. Gardner's foreword to Frank S. Edwards's *A Campaign in New Mexico with Colonel Doniphan* (Albuquerque, 1996), xii–xiv. Turner was clearly engaged in mythmaking. While Magoffin's activities in Santa Fe in August of 1846 furthered Kearny's aim of a peaceful occupation of New Mexico, the military was under orders from the Polk administration to conquer New Mexico without bloodshed, and that is what they reported that they accomplished. Yet resistance on the part of New Mexicans took various forms. Most notable were the December plot of 1846, a failed attempt by leading citizens—merchants, politicians, and clergy—to overthrow Kearny's occupation government, and the Taos rebellion of 1847, which cost Governor Charles Bent his life. Some two hundred New Mexicans fell in battle against United States troops during January and February 1847. Not a drop of blood was spilled in August 1846 in Santa Fe, thanks to the good offices of James Magoffin, but it flowed freely after he left the scene and was in a Mexican prison, a fact he acknowledged after the war. Tobias Duran, "We Came as Friends: Violent Social Conflict in New Mexico, 1810–1910," (Ph.D. diss., University of New Mexico, 1985), 48; Martín González de la Vara, *México y Estados Unidos: Orígenes de una relación, 1819–1981* (Mexico City, 1987), 133.

9. Lamar, *The Far Southwest*, 63.

10. Timmons, *El Paso*, 93; Drumm, *Down the Santa Fe Trail*, 108.

11. Timmons, *El Paso*, 93.

12. Drumm, *Down the Santa Fe Trail*, 169.

13. Charles M. Haecker, "Brazito Battlefield: Once Lost Now Found," *New Mexico Historical Review* 72 (July 1997): 231; Neil C. Mangum, "The Battle of Brazito: Reappraising a Lost and Forgotten Episode in the Mexican-American War," *New Mexico Historical Review* 72 (July 1997): 225. For additional insights, including material from often neglected Mexican sources, see Enrique Tamez Vasquez, "Brazito Remembered One Hundred Fifty Years Ago: Another Look," *Password* 43 (summer 1998): 55–68.

14. Timmons, *El Paso*, 95.

15. When President Polk learned of the American victory at Sacramento, he said, "I consider it to be the most decisive and brilliant achievement of the War." Gibson, *Journey of a Soldier*, 102.

16. Twitchell, *The Conquest of Santa Fe*, 58.

17. Ibid, 52–54.

18. Moorhead, *New Mexico's Royal Road*, 183.

19. Strickland, *Six Who Came to El Paso*, 29.

CHAPTER FIVE

1. Timmons, "The El Paso Area in the Mexican Period," 24–27.

2. Ibid., 26–27.

3. W. H. Timmons, "American El Paso: The Formative Years, 1848–1858," *Southwestern Historical Quarterly* 87 (July 1983): 3.

4. Ibid., 5.

5. Paul Horgan, *Great River: The Rio Grande in North American History* (New York, 1954), 2:802–3; John Russell Bartlett, *Personal Narrative of Explorations and Incidents in Texas, New Mexico, California, Sonora, and Chihuahua* (New York, 1854), 1:193.

6. Strickland, *Six Who Came to El Paso*, 27; Drumm, *Down the Santa Fe Trail*, xix .

7. Baylor, *Into the Far, Wild Country*, 138.

8. Of the many disputes involving land titles in the territory acquired from Mexico in 1848, the Canutillo grant was one of the most important, and Magoffin did not receive full title until 1858. Bowden, *Spanish and Mexican Land Grants*, 95–97; Strickland, *Six Who Came to El Paso*, 29–30; J. W. Magoffin to José Cordero, 1849, Magoffin-Cordero Papers, Magoffin Home.

9. J. W. Magoffin to the Committee of El Paso County, 5 August 1852, Governors' Papers: Peter H. Bell, Texas State Archives, Austin. See Documentary Appendix.

10. Hugh Stephenson et al. to Millard Fillmore, 20 December 1851, Governors' Papers: Peter H. Bell.

11. Timmons, "American El Paso: The Formative Years," 34.

12. Strickland, *Six Who Came to El Paso*, 30–32.

13. Ibid.

14. Rex W. Strickland, *El Paso in 1854* (El Sabio Sembrador *by Frederick Augustus Percy*) (El Paso, 1969), 39.

15. Nancy Lee Hammons, *A History of El Paso County, Texas, to 1900* (El Paso, 1983), 41.

16. Ibid., 40.

17. Ibid.; Harlan D. Fowler, *Camels to California* (Stanford, 1950), 55–57; Lewis Burt Lesley, ed., *Uncle Sam's Camels: The Journal of May Humphreys Stacey, Supplemented by the Report of Edward Fitzgerald Beale, 1857–1858* (Cambridge, Mass., 1929), 170–71.

18. Lydia Spenser Lane, *I Married a Soldier* (Albuquerque, 1964), 68.

19. Strickland, *El Paso in 1854*, 27, 43; William W. H. Davis, *El Gringo; or, New Mexico and Her People* (New York, 1857), 377.

CHAPTER SIX

1. Bartlett, *Personal Narrative*, 2:435–37; Moorhead, *New Mexico's Royal*

Road, 76–82, 156; Gardner, *Brothers on the Santa Fe and Chihuahua Trails*, 137–38 n. 1.

2. Francisco R. Almada, *Diccionario de historia, geografía y biografía chihuahuenses* (Ciudad Juárez, 1968), 117.

3. Moorhead, *New Mexico's Royal Road*, 180 n. 68; Gardner, *Brothers on the Santa Fe and Chihuahua Trails*, 157 n. 114.

4. James Josiah Webb, *Adventures in the Santa Fe Trade, 1844–47*, ed. Ralph P. Bieber (Glendale, Calif., 1931), 277–78; Hubert Howe Bancroft, *North Mexican States and Texas* (San Francisco, 1889), 2:617.

5. Bartlett, *Personal Narrative*, 2:435–37.

6. José Cordero to Santiago Magoffin, August 1850, Magoffin-Cordero Papers.

7. Isaac Lightner to Magoffin, 8 October 1853, Magoffin-Cordero Papers.

8. Lightner to Magoffin, 18 April 1854, Magoffin-Cordero Papers.

9. Francisco Elguea to Magoffin, 13 June 1850, Magoffin-Cordero Papers.

10. Elguea to Magoffin, 3 November 1853; Elguea to Magoffin, 13 April 1854; Elguea to Magoffin, 28 November 1854, Magoffin-Cordero Papers.

11. Magoffin to Cordero, 22 March 1857, Magoffin-Cordero Papers.

12. The financial records of the Magoffin-Cordero partnership cover thirteen pages, all written in a legible hand. In view of Moorhead's comment that "only a few of the traders' ledgers have survived," the Magoffin-Cordero records constitute a major historical discovery. Moorhead, *New Mexico's Royal Road*, 186.

13. Timmons, *El Paso*, 153.

14. Samuel E. Bell and James M. Smallwood, *The Zona Libre, 1858–1905* (El Paso, 1982), 1–17.

15. David R. Diffenderfer to Lewis Cass, El Paso del Norte, 10 April 1858, Despatches from United States Consuls in Ciudad Juárez (microfilm, UTEP Library, M184R1).

16. James Magoffin to Gov. Sam Houston, Magoffinsville, 24 May 1860, Governors' Papers: Sam Houston, Box 3-1-32 (53).

17. United States Census, El Paso County, 1860 (microfilm, UTEP Library, MF1621/M653).

18. Timmons, *El Paso*, 154.

Chapter Seven

1. W. F. Smith, *Report of Routes from San Antonio to El Paso*, Sen. Exec. Doc. 64, 31st Cong., 1st sess. (1850), serial set 562, 50.

2. Randolph B. Marcy, *Report of a Route from Fort Smith to Santa Fe*, Sen. Exec. Doc. 129, 33rd Cong., 1st sess. (1855), serial set 737, 43–44.

3. Ibid.

4. Wayne R. Austerman, *Sharps Rifles and Spanish Mules* (College Station, Tex., 1985), 46.

5. Timmons, *El Paso*, 129.

6. Ibid., 129–31.

7. Samuel Magoffin to James Magoffin, St. Louis County, 24 August 1854, Glasgow Collection.

8. Samuel Magoffin to James Magoffin, St. Louis, 8 April 1855, Glasgow Collection.

9. Samuel Magoffin to Isaac Lightner, 15 December 1855, Glasgow Collection.

10. L. R. Bailey, ed., *The A. B. Gray Report* (Los Angeles, 1963), 43–46; S. G. Reed, *A History of the Texas Railroads* (Houston, 1941), 98–99.

11. J. Morgan Broaddus, *The Legal Heritage of El Paso* (El Paso, 1963), 64–65.

12. John C. Reid, *Reid's Tramp, Or A Journal of the Incidents of Ten Months' Travel Through Texas, New Mexico, Arizona, Sonora, and California* (1858; reprint, Austin, 1935), 139–50.

13. Ibid., 151–54.

14. Davis, *El Gringo*, 380.

15. Rex W. Strickland, ed., *Forty Years at El Paso, 1858–1898, by W. W. Mills* (El Paso, 1962), 28. Quoted in Timmons, *El Paso*, 146.

CHAPTER EIGHT

1. Timmons, *El Paso*, 146–47.

2. Ibid.

3. Martin Hardwick Hall, *Sibley's New Mexico Campaign* (Austin, 1960), 20–21.

4. J. W. Magoffin to Gov. Edward Clark, Fort Bliss, 28 April 1861, Governors' Papers: Edward Clark, Box 301–32 53.

5. J. F. Crosby to Gov. Edward Clark, El Paso, 9 May 1861, Governors' Papers: Edward Clark.

6. Hall, *Sibley's New Mexico Campaign*, 26.

7. Austerman, *Sharps Rifles and Spanish Mules*, 182.

8. Hall, *Sibley's New Mexico Campaign*, 28.

9. Ibid., 29–30; Timmons, *El Paso*, 148.

10. Donald S. Frazier, *Blood and Treasure: Confederate Empire in the Southwest* (College Station, Tex., 1995), 76–78.

11. Ibid.; United States War Department, *Confederate Victories in the Southwest: Prelude to Defeat* (Albuquerque, 1961), 113.

12. Hall, *Sibley's New Mexico Campaign*, 45–46.

13. Robert Lee Kerby, *The Confederate Invasion of New Mexico and Arizona, 1861–1862* (Los Angeles, 1958), 61–62.

14. Ibid., 79–80.

15. Hall, *Sibley's New Mexico Campaign*, 55.

16. Timmons, *El Paso*, 148–50; Jerry Thompson, *Henry Hopkins Sibley: Confederate General of the West* (Natchitoches, La., 1987), 306.

17. Timmons, *El Paso*, 150.

18. Ibid.

19. Dolores V. de Magoffin to Sr. Don Luis Valdez, El Paso del Norte, 14 July 1862, Juárez Archive (microfilm, UTEP Library, MF495R64F2–3).

20. Luis Valdez to Don Santiago Magoffin, El Paso del Norte, 18 July 1862, Glasgow Collection.

21. "Joseph Magoffin," Magoffin Family File, in the Pioneers' Sketch Book, Harrodsburg Historical Society.

22. Augustus B. O'Bannon to James Magoffin, 25 July 1865, Glasgow Collection.

23. Robert Ryal Miller, *Arms across the Border: United States Aid to Juárez during the French Intervention in Mexico* (Philadelphia, 1973), 7.

24. *Santa Fe Gazette*, 2 September 1865; John William Draper, *History of the American Civil War* (New York, 1868), 2:171, 184. See Documentary Appendix.

25. A. J. Hamilton to J. W. Magoffin, 13 November 1865, Governors' Papers: A. J. Hamilton; J. W. Magoffin to Gov. A. J. Hamilton, San Antonio, 6 December 1865, Governors' Papers: A. J. Hamilton.

26. President Andrew Johnson, Pardon of James W. Magoffin, 7 September 1867, Center for Southwest Studies, University of New Mexico Library. See Documentary Appendix.

27. Darlis A. Miller, *Soldiers and Settlers* (Albuquerque, 1989), 218.

28. Lane, *I Married a Soldier*, 170.

29. Strickland, *Six Who Came to El Paso*, 34. Magoffin's Mexican partner, José Cordero, died in September 1867, leaving an estate amounting to more than six hundred thousand dollars. Almada, *Diccionario de historia*, 117–18.

CONCLUSION

1. *Magoffin Home State Historic Site* (Austin, 1994).

BIBLIOGRAPHY

PRIMARY SOURCES

A. Manuscript Collections

Archivo del Ayuntamiento de Chihuahua. University of Texas at El Paso (UTEP) Library, El Paso.

Bartlett, John Russell. Papers. The Mexican Boundary Commission Correspondence, 1850–1853. UTEP Library.

Béxar Archives. University of Texas at Austin Library, Austin.

Biographical and Historical Sketchbook of the Pioneers' Association of El Paso County, 1932. UTEP Library.

Despatches from United States Consuls in Ciudad Juárez. UTEP Library.

Despatches from United States Consuls in Matamoros. UTEP Library.

El Paso County Deed Book D. C. L. Sonnichsen Special Collections Department. UTEP Library.

Federal Census of 1860. UTEP Library.

General Records of the Department of State. Center for Southwest Studies. University of New Mexico Library, Albuquerque.

Glasgow, Mrs. W. J. Collection. Magoffin Home, El Paso, Texas.

Governors' Papers: Bell, Clark, Hamilton, Houston. Texas State Archives, Austin.

Juárez Archive. UTEP Library.

Magoffin, James W., and José Cordero Papers. Magoffin Home.

National Archives, Consulate General, Mexican Correspondence, Washington, D.C.

New Mexico State Records Center and Archives, Santa Fe.

B. Published Documents

Almonte, Juan N. "Statistical Report on Texas." Translated by C. E. Castañeda. *Southwestern Historical Quarterly* 28 (January 1925): 177–221.

Bailey, L. R., ed. *The A. B. Gray Report*. Los Angeles: Westernlore Press, 1963.

Bartlett, John Russell. *Personal Narrative of Travel and Incidents in Texas, New Mexico, California, Sonora, and Chihuahua*. 2 vols. New York: Appleton Co., 1854.

Benton, Thomas Hart. *Thirty Years' View*. New York: D. Appleton and Co., 1856.

Cooke, Philip St. George. *The Conquest of New Mexico and California in 1846–1848*. Albuquerque: Horn and Wallace, Publishers, 1964.

Davis, William W. H. *El Gringo; or, New Mexico and Her People*. New York: Harper Bros., 1857.

Drumm, Stella M., ed. *Down the Santa Fe Trail and into Mexico: Diary of Susan Shelby Magoffin, 1846–1847*. New Haven: Yale University Press, 1926.

Edwards, Frank S. *A Campaign in New Mexico with Colonel Doniphan*. Foreword by Mark L. Gardner. Albuquerque: University of New Mexico Press, 1996.

El Paso Trouble in Texas. House Exec. Doc. No. 93. 45th Cong., 2nd sess.

Gardner, Mark L., ed. *Brothers on the Santa Fe and Chihuahua Trails*. Niwot, Colo.: University Press of Colorado, 1993.

Gardner, Mark L., and Marc Simmons, eds. *The Mexican War Correspondence of Richard Smith Elliot*. Norman, Okla.: University of Oklahoma Press, 1997.

Gibson, George Rutledge. *Journal of a Soldier Under Kearny and Doniphan, 1846–1847*. Edited by Ralph P. Bieber. Glendale, Calif.: Arthur H. Clark Co., 1935.

Jenkins, John H., ed. *The Papers of the Texas Revolution, 1835–36*. 10 vols. Austin: Presidial Press, 1973.

Lane, Lydia Spenser. *I Married a Soldier*. Albuquerque: University of New Mexico Press, 1964.

Lesley, Lewis Burt, ed. *Uncle Sam's Camels: The Journal of May Humphreys Stacey, Supplemented by the Report of Edward Fitzgerald Beale, 1857–1858*. Cambridge, Mass.: Harvard

University Press, 1929.

Marcy, Randolph B. *Report of a Route from Fort Smith to Santa Fe.* Sen. Exec. Doc. 129, 33rd Cong., 1st sess. (1855), serial set 737.

Morgan, Dale, ed. *Overland in 1846.* 2 vols. Georgetown, Calif.: The Talisman Press, 1963.

Pope, John. *Report of Explorations of a Route for the Pacific Railroad.* House Exec. Doc. 129, 33rd Cong., 1st sess. (1855), serial set 737.

Reid, John C. *Reid's Tramp, Or A Journal of the Incidents of Ten Months' Travel Through Texas, New Mexico, Arizona, Sonora, and California.* 1858. Reprint, Austin: The Steck Co., 1935.

Santa Fe Gazette. 2 September 1865.

Strickland, Rex W., ed. *Forty Years at El Paso 1858–1898 by W. W. Mills.* El Paso: Carl Hertzog, 1962.

——. *El Paso in 1854* (El Sabio Sembrador *by Frederick Augustus Percy*). El Paso: Texas Western Press, 1969.

The Territorial Papers of the United States. Vols. 6, 18I, 19. Washington, D.C., 1938.

Twitchell, Ralph Emerson. *The Conquest of Santa Fe.* Edited by Bill Tate. Truchas, N. Mex.: Tate Gallery, 1967.

United States War Department. *Confederate Victories in the Southwest: Prelude to Defeat.* Albuquerque: Horn & Wallace, Publishers, 1961.

Webb, James Josiah. *Adventures in the Santa Fe Trade, 1844–1847.* Edited by Ralph P. Bieber. Southwest Historical Series, no. 1. Glendale, Calif.: Arthur H. Clark Co., 1931.

Wislizenus, A. *Memoir of a Tour to Northern Mexico Connected with Colonel Doniphan's Expedition in 1846 and 1847.* Albuquerque: Calvin Horn Publisher, Inc., 1969.

II. Secondary Materials

A. Books

Almada, Francisco R. *Diccionario de historia, geografía y biografía chihuahuenses.* Ciudad Juárez: El Impresor de Juárez, 1968.

Altamirano, Graziella, and Guadalupe Villa. *Chihuahua: Textos de su historia, 1824–1921*. Vol. 1. Mexico City: Gobierno del Estado de Chihuahua, Instituto de Investigaciones Dr. José María Luis Mora, and Universidad Autónima de Ciudad Juárez, 1988., 1:339.

Austerman, Wayne R. *Sharps Rifles and Spanish Mules*. College Station, Tex.: Texas A&M Press, 1985.

Bancroft, Hubert Howe. *History of the North Mexican States and Texas*. 2 vols. San Francisco: The History Company, 1884–1885.

Barker, Eugene C. *The Life of Stephen F. Austin*. Dallas: Cokesbury Press, 1925.

———. *Mexico and Texas, 1821–1835*. Dallas: P. L. Turner Co., 1928.

Baylor, George Wythe. *Into the Far, Wild Country*. Edited by Jerry D. Thompson. El Paso: Texas Western Press, 1996.

Beachum, Larry Mahon. *William Becknell: Father of the Santa Fe Trade*. Southwestern Studies, no. 68. El Paso: Texas Western Press, 1982.

Bell, Samuel E., and James M. Smallwood. *The Zona Libre, 1858–1905*. Southwestern Studies, no. 69. El Paso: Texas Western Press, 1982.

Bowden, J. J. *Spanish and Mexican Land Grants in the Chihuahuan Acquisition*. El Paso: Texas Western Press, 1971.

Broaddus, J. Morgan. *The Legal Heritage of El Paso*. El Paso: Texas Western Press, 1963.

Castañeda, Carlos E. *Our Catholic Heritage in Texas*. 7 vols. Austin: Von Boeckman–Jones Co., 1936–1958.

Chalfant, William Y. *Dangerous Passage: The Santa Fe Trail and the Mexican War*. Norman, Okla.: University of Oklahoma Press, 1994.

Clark, Thomas D. *A History of Kentucky*. Lexington, Ky.: The John Bradford Press, 1960.

———. *The Kentucky*. New York: Farrar and Rinehart, 1942.

Connelley, William Elsey. *Doniphan's Expedition*. Kansas City: Bryant and Douglas Co., 1907.

Draper, John William. *History of the American Civil War*. Vol. 1. New York: Harper Brothers, 1868.

Duffus, R. I. *The Santa Fe Trail*. New York: Longmans, Green Co., 1930.

Fowler, Harlan D. *Camels to California*. Stanford: Stanford University Press, 1950.

Frazier, Donald S. *Blood and Treasure: Confederate Empire in the Southwest*. College Station, Tex.: Texas A&M Press, 1995.

González de la Vara, Martín. *México y Estados Unidos: Orígenes de una relación, 1819–1981*. Mexico City: Secretaría de Educación Pública, 1987.

Gould, E. W. *Fifty Years on the Mississippi*. St. Louis: Nixon-Jones Printing Co., 1889.

Griffen, William B. *Utmost Good Faith: Patterns of Apache-Mexican Hostilities in Northern Chihuahua Border Warfare, 1821–1848*. Albuquerque: University of New Mexico Press, 1988.

Hall, Martin Hardwick. *Sibley's New Mexico Campaign*. Austin: University of Texas Press, 1960.

Hamilton, Nancy. *Ben Dowell: El Paso's First Mayor*. Southwestern Studies, no. 49. El Paso: Texas Western Press, 1976.

Hammons, Nancy Lee. *A History of El Paso County, Texas, to 1900*. El Paso: University of Texas at El Paso, 1983.

Hendricks, Rick, and W. H. Timmons. *San Elizario: Spanish Presidio to Texas County Seat*. El Paso: Texas Western Press, 1998.

Horgan, Paul. *Great River: The Rio Grande in North American History*. 2 vols. New York: Rinehart and Co., 1954.

Kerby, Robert Lee. *The Confederate Invasion of New Mexico and Arizona, 1861–1862*. Los Angeles: Westernlore Press, 1958.

Kincaid, Robert L. *The Wilderness Road*. Indianapolis: Bobbs-Merrill Co., 1947.

King, Grace. *New Orleans: The Place and the People*. New York: Negro University Press, 1968.

Lamar, Howard Roberts. *The Far Southwest, 1846–1912: A Territorial History*. New Haven: Yale University Press, 1966.

Lea, Tom. *The King Ranch*. 2 vols. Boston: Little, Brown Co., 1957.

Loomis, Noel M. *The Texan–Santa Fe Pioneers*. Norman, Okla.: University of Oklahoma Press, 1958.

McCandless, Perry. *A History of Missouri*. 2 vols. Columbia, Mo.: University of Missouri Press, 1972.

Miller, Darlis A. *Soldiers and Settlers*. Albuquerque: University of New Mexico Press, 1989.

Miller, Robert Ryal. *Arms across the Border: United States Aid to Juárez during the French Intervention in Mexico*. Philadelphia: American Philosophical Society, 1973.

Moorhead, Max L. *New Mexico's Royal Road*. Norman, Okla.: University of Oklahoma Press, 1958.

Morton, Ohland. *Terán and Texas*. Austin: The Texas State Historical Association, 1948.

Reed, S. G. *A History of Texas Railroads*. Houston: The St. Clair Publishing Co., 1941.

Simmons, Marc. *On the Santa Fe Trail*. Lawrence, Kans.: University Press of Kansas, 1986.

Smithwick, Noah. *The Evolution of a State*. Austin: The Steck Co., 1935.

Strickland, Rex. *Six Who Came to El Paso: Pioneers of the 1840s*. Southwestern Studies, no. 3. El Paso: Texas Western Press, 1963.

Swift, Roy L., and Leavitt Corning Jr. *Three Roads to Chihuahua*. Austin: Eakin Press, 1998.

Thompson, Jerry D. *Henry Hopkins Sibley: Confederate General of the West*. Natchitoches, La.: Northwestern State University Press, 1987.

Timmons, W. H. *El Paso: A Borderlands History*. El Paso: Texas Western Press, 1990.

Weber, David J. *The Mexican Frontier*. Albuquerque: University of New Mexico Press, 1982.

B. Articles

Baylor, George Wythe. "Tales of Don Santiago." *El Paso Herald*. 20 January 1900.

Bowden, J. J. "The Magoffin Salt War." *Password* 7 (summer 1962): 95–121.

Brown, R. B. "John Potts of Chihuahua." *Password* 43 (spring 1998): 3–13.

Haecker, Charles M. "Brazito Battlefield: Once Lost Now Found." *New Mexico Historical Review* 72 (July 1997): 229–38.

Howren, Alleine. "Causes and Origins of the Decree of April 6, 1830." *Southwestern Historical Quarterly* 16 (April 1913): 378–422.

Lucker, Josephine Magoffin. "Memories of the Magoffin Homestead." *Password* 20 (spring 1975): 11–16.

Mangum, Neil C. "The Battle of Brazito: Reappraising a Lost and Forgotten Episode in the Mexican-American War." *New Mexico Historical Review* 72 (July 1997): 217–28.

Porter, Eugene O. "The Great Flood of 1897." *Password* 18 (fall 1973): 95–103.

Tamez Vasquez, Enrique. "Brazito Remembered One Hundred Fifty Years Ago: Another Look." *Password* 43 (summer 1998): 55–68.

Timmons, W. H. "Joseph Magoffin Materials in the Juárez Archive." *Password* 23 (winter 1978): 129–34.

———. "The El Paso Area in the Mexican Period, 1821–1848." *Southwestern Historical Quarterly* 84 (July 1980): 1–28.

———. "American El Paso: The Formative Years, 1848–1858," *Southwestern Historical Quarterly* 86 (July 1983): 1–36.

Wagner, Frank. "John Stryker." *The New Handbook of Texas*. 6 vols. Austin: Texas State Historical Association, 1996.

Waller, John L. "James Wiley Magoffin." *The Handbook of Texas*. Edited by Walter Prescott Webb. Vol. 2. Austin: Texas State Historical Association, 1962.

Wise, Clyde, Jr., "The Effects of the Railroads upon El Paso." *Password* 5 (July 1960): 91–100.

C. Pamphlets

Magoffin Home State Historic Site. Austin: Texas Parks and Wildlife Department, 1994.

D. Unpublished Material

Crego, Arthur VanHorhis. "City of the Mesa—The New Fort Bliss." Typed manuscript in C. L. Sonnichsen Special Collections Department, UTEP Library.

Duran, Tobias. "We Came as Friends: Violent Social Conflict in New Mexico, 1810–1910." Ph.D. diss., University of New Mexico, 1985.

Freeman, Leola. "James Wiley Magoffin." Typed manuscript in author's possession, 1951.

INDEX